How to Get Your Car Repaired without Getting Gypped

How to Get Your Car Repaired without Getting Gypped

MARGARET BRESNAHAN CARLSON
with Ronald G. Shafer

Harper & Row, Publishers
New York, Evanston, San Francisco, London

LIBRARY OF CONGRESS CATALOG CARD NUMBER: 72–11811

STANDARD BOOK NUMBER: 06–010612–3 (Cloth)
06–463341–1 (Paper)

Contents

22631

Part Three: Where to Go

Part Four: How to Protect Yourself

Part Five: How to Get Your Car Fixed Right,
    or Get Your Money Back

Introduction

Owning an automobile may be the American dream, but keeping it repaired can be a never-ending nightmare. Americans pay out more than $29 billion a year to service and repair over 110 million vehicles. A Senate subcommittee, after a three-year investigation into the auto repair industry, estimates $10 billion of this is wasted on shoddy, unneeded, or overpriced repairs.

Testimony at the Senate hearings of the Subcommittee on Antitrust and Monopoly from automobile company executives, insurance officials, mechanics, and corporate critics painted a picture of a repair system replete with greed, overpricing, lack of regulation, incompetence, and monopolistic control. The system not only bilks the individual car owner but the public at large by returning poorly repaired and unsafe vehicles to the road.

"It was clear that the consumer who got his car fixed right the first try may be just plain lucky," concluded Senator Philip A. Hart, the Michigan Democrat who chaired the Senate hearings.

The problem is getting worse. Virginia Knauer, President Nixon's Special Assistant for Consumer Affairs, reports that "by far the highest percentage of consumer complaints received in my office each month pertain to automobiles. . . . A common thread seems to run through a great many of them—the problem of servicing."

A nationwide poll of consumer views made in early

1972 for *Life* magazine by Louis Harris & Associates, Inc., concluded that "In the case of automotive repairs, the level of complaints in the five-year period from 1967 to 1972 has risen alarmingly." The Harris poll showed more and more car owners complain that their auto repairs aren't made properly, that costs for repairs are excessive, and that unneeded repairs are made. The 1972 results and those of a similar Harris poll made in 1967 are shown below:

AUTO REPAIRS	HAPPENS FREQUENTLY OR FAIRLY OFTEN		CHANGE
	1972	*1967*	
Made improperly	31%	16%	up 15%
Repeat failures	32%	17%	up 15%
Unnecessary repairs	19%	6%	up 13%
Excess costs	41%	19%	up 22%

In days gone by, the automobile was a fairly simple machine that even the least mechanically minded could understand. But in today's world of automatic transmissions, 350-horsepower engines, and retractable headlights, a car is a complex creature whose inner workings few of us can comprehend.

If you're like most motorists, the bad news from your friendly neighborhood mechanic that the family chariot is in dire need of some complicated-sounding repairs leaves you with only two choices: Either you pretend to understand what he's talking about and pay for repairs you're not really sure you need, or you get smart, demand a detailed mechanical explanation—and *then* pay for repairs you're not sure you really need.

This book was written for the great nonmechanical majority who don't know much about how their cars work and aren't interested enough to find out, but who want to keep their cars in decent operating condition without too much trouble and expense.

Even if you don't know a carburetor from a distributor cap, there are ways to cut through the auto repair maze of complexities, incompetence, and dishonesty. This book is designed to give you an understanding of how the repair system works and a healthy dose of tactics to deal with it.

Part one describes some common frauds, like "skinning the dude" and the "escalating estimate," that you should be on guard against. The best safeguard, as outlined in part two, is to determine in advance what repairs actually may be needed. Unfortunately, the local mechanic can't be treated like the family doctor. Simply say, "My car is sick, make it well," and you're likely to find yourself at the mercy of a lazy or dishonest repairman who will start replacing parts until he happens to hit on the right cure. But if you can go to a mechanic and say, "The car is running roughly, check the air filter and adjust the carburetor," you'll get better service.

If your car is getting along in mileage, a parallel concern is whether the repairs are worth making. It's hard to tell when a car has reached the point of no return, but there are clues. Once past that point, you can invest $300 in an engine overhaul only to be faced with one repair bill after another in the following weeks.

The next important question is, where to go? This is discussed in part three. The auto repair system consists of over 400,000 outlets—new-car dealers, independent garages, specialty shops, mass merchandisers, and service stations. Each has its weaknesses and advantages. For example, you might find it cheaper to buy a new battery at a mass merchandiser such as Sears Roebuck, Montgomery Ward, and J. C. Penney because they can buy batteries wholesale at larger volume discounts than an independent garage or service station. And since installing a battery is easy, a highly trained mechanic isn't necessary.

If your car is under warranty, the new-car dealer might be the easy answer to the question of where to go for repairs. But if it's a slow day or the mechanic feels he's losing money on warranty work, he may find extra repairs and charge you for them. There was a time when gas stations only pumped gas. Now, many perform major repairs. A competent gas station mechanic can be worth his weight in gold-plated monkey wrenches. But mistaking a friendly gas jockey for a knowledgeable mechanic can cost you trouble and money.

Once you've decided where to take your car, there are things you should know to protect yourself. Part four of this book tells you how to decipher the standard repair order, how to determine proper labor charges, and how to preserve your legal rights in case the job isn't done right.

Finally, part five explains the tactics you can use either to get an unsatisfactory repair redone correctly or to get your money back. You can complain loudly, write letters, or just sulk. Or you can go to small claims court. Very few do. But those who take that legal step win more than 50 percent of the time. And you don't even need a lawyer.

The car owner has long been victimized by those garage owners or mechanics who will take advantage of his (or, especially, her) helplessness. But by learning a few key defenses, you can make it a whole new ball game.

part one ─────────────────

Is This Repair Really Necessary? Common Frauds to Watch Out For

chapter 1 ─────────────

Trapping the Traveler

The gas gauge on the Michigan coed's compact car was nearing empty, so she wheeled off the next freeway exit and into the nearest service station. One hour and $225 later she drove out of the station with two new tires and a host of new auto parts, none of which she really needed.

What happened? The coed had driven into a not uncommon trap: highway service stations that specialize in scare tactics, and even calculated vandalism, to push auto parts and accessories on cautious travelers.

It all seemed innocent enough to the coed. The station attendant filled her car's gas tank and checked the oil and the tires. Five minutes after pulling into the station, she turned the key to start the engine. Nothing happened. The car wouldn't move.

Fortunately, the service station attendant was a helpful fellow. Rushing to the young girl's rescue, he checked under the hood and soon spotted the problem. The battery was dead, the generator was shot, and the fuel pump was leaking. What's more, he noticed that her car's two front tires seemed to be losing air. The car certainly wasn't in any shape to get very far safely.

The coed didn't know what a generator was, much less a fuel pump. But she knew she was anxious to get going and certainly didn't want to get stuck on the road. She waited while the friendly attendant put on two new tires, a battery, a generator, and a fuel pump and then charged the bill on her credit card.

After arriving home, the coed had her car checked by a mechanic friend. He discovered that, except for the tires, none of the supposedly malfunctioning items had been replaced at all and the old parts were still working fine. Indications were that the friendly service station attendant had created the road repair emergency by disconnecting the battery cables, squirting oil on the fuel pump, and probably puncturing the tires. Then, figuring he had a real pigeon lady on his hands, he had charged for repairs which he hadn't bothered to make.

Traveling motorists, easily identified by their out-of-state license plates, are special targets for the high-pressure sales tactics of fraudulent repair operations. Away from home and anxious to be on their way, such travelers are less likely to be in a position to question the need for a costly repair.

"Prime targets of the fraudulent operators are motorists with out-of-state licenses, women traveling alone or with children and individuals unfamiliar with the English language," the California attorney general said after a probe by his office into frauds in that state.

Nobody knows how much fraudulent auto repairs cost U.S. motorists, but investigations by the attorneys general of California and Arizona documented annual losses of millions of dollars from service station frauds. Indeed, California officials in 1972 estimated that in San Bernardino County alone consumers were being bilked out of more than $2 million a year on the desert road to Las Vegas. Interstate 15, the desert highway between Las Vegas and Barstow, California, has long been considered a major area for service station highway robbery. Other trouble spots have been Route 66 in Arizona and Route 95 in Florida.

The following are some of the common frauds you are likely to encounter both at home and away, but especially on the road. Some are perpetrated by supposedly reputable businesses who feel such practices are necessary to assure a reasonable profit. Others are the work of outright con artists for whom the garage is a front for their bunco operations.

The Gypsy Gas Station

The gypsy gas station frequently is marked by a prominently placed "Last Chance for Gas" sign. Usually located on the outskirts of a city, it is passed off as the last mark of civilization. Its major purpose: pushing needless repairs on the motorist about to get onto the freeway. After checking under the hood, the mechanic will tell you how lucky you are that you stopped, that it just so happens you need spark plugs, points, and a condenser. All this is especially effective if you are anxious to get where you are going.

To avoid becoming a victim of such tactics, remember: No mechanic can tell by just looking under the hood that you need new points, plugs, or condenser. And, before undertaking a trip, have the car checked in your home city, making yourself less vulnerable to the gypsy station.

Skinning the Dude

The tactics of the gypsy station are rather harmless compared to the repair tricks uncovered by the Los Angeles police department and the attorneys general of California, Arizona, and several East Coast states. They found that service stations under the signs of some of the nation's largest chains were not only using high-pressure scare tactics and fast talk to push parts and repairs but were also engaging in a sly sabotage, known in the trade as "skinning the dude."

Almost before you can say "fill 'er up," sharpies at these stations, known as "tool men," can loosen a battery cable, cut a fan belt, or puncture a radiator hose. They're also accomplished at slashing, or "honking," tires or giving the "shock treatment" by pouring oil on the engine to make it look defective—anything to get the car up on the rack and into their clutches.

When traveling, the motorist should remember that where there's smoke there isn't always fire. A common trick of service station con artists is to squirt some titanium tetrachloride, a meat curative, on your car's alternator (or generator) from a syringe hidden beneath an oil rag. The result: lots of white smoke and, too often, up to a $90 repair bill for a new alternator. (Other slick operators may create smoke simply by pouring barbecue sauce on a hot engine.)

The "fire," however, is harmless. Simply by sniffing you may be able to smell a rat because the smoke from the meat curative doesn't smell like smoke from a fire. A better check: turn your ignition key (without cranking the engine). If the alternator light goes on, the phony fix is on too. (On many cars the alternator warning light—as well as the oil pressure light—goes on when you turn the key and quickly goes off when the engine starts unless something is wrong. On other cars, the alternator gauge shows whether the system is charging or discharging—a sharp, continuing discharge when the engine is running means problems.)

Another under-the-hood trick is to bend the alternator wires to activate the warning light. If the light wasn't flashing before you drove in (or discharging with a charge-discharge gauge), chances are the light shouldn't be flashing now unless the alternator has been purposely short-circuited. You won't get far with a bum alternator, but you can probably drive to another station if one is nearby.

Sudden battery trouble may be traced to an Alka Seltzer tablet plunked into a battery cell. This neutralizes the cell and causes it to boil over. The damage may or may not be permanent. If you do buy a new battery, insist on keeping the old one so you can have it checked later to see if it was tampered with.

Leaking shock absorbers are another common ploy. The attendant squirts crankcase oil on a shock absorber and then helpfully reports that you need new shocks. Take a look at the leaking shock absorber (shocks are the four tubelike devices under the car by each wheel). If the oil starts in the middle, the leak is a fake. Real shock absorber leaks start at the top, but—with the car sitting on the ground—the attendant can't reach that point with his oiler.

If you have less than 20,000 miles on your present

shocks, it's unlikely you need new ones. At any rate, a leaking shock absorber isn't an emergency, so you can have it checked later.

"Short sticking" is another popular ploy of the gas station con artists. With this trick the attendant checks your oil, but pushes the dipstick down only part way. Result: the dipstick, which the attendant dutifully shows you, indicates that you are low a quart of oil. He then sells you his most expensive brand. To top off his trickery, he often will then "pour" an empty can of oil into your crankcase.

The incentive for attendants to engage in these shenanigans is that at such stations they are hired on the basis of up to a 50 percent cut of the profits on all parts and oil they can peddle to customers. In the San Bernardino, California, area, some experienced "fifty-percenters" were reported to be making from $1000 to $4000 a month.

The best safeguard against "skinning the dude" is a simple one: get out of the car when you stop for gas. Even the boldest tool man isn't likely to pull his stunts with you looking over his shoulder.

Another way to avoid being "skinned"—after being suddenly told you need a repair—is to get a second opinion at the station down the road. But on some highways even this isn't a sure protection. "When the San Bernardino county sheriff conducted a one-day investigation of the main stations along the desert road," reported the White House Office of Consumer Affairs, "he found that in two-thirds of the stations attendants were carrying such tools of the cheater's trade as barbecue sauce, or spikes for puncturing tires."

Freeway Runners

Some gas stations aren't satisfied to leave the finding of pigeons to chance. They send out "freeway runners," drivers who go along the freeway, pull alongside a car and, in a neighborly fashion, signal that your tire looks low or it's wobbling. In many cases, the sucker pulls off at the next exit, an easy mark for the intended gas station.

Tire Tricks

Police in California, where automobiles are a way of life, have an active fraud detail complete with undercover cars and mechanics. What the investigators uncovered was a tire-selling operation in freeway gas stations bordering on highway robbery. With slight variations the operation goes like this: You pull in for gas. You've got out-of-state license plates, a car full of kids, and you look like you're on vacation. The sharp salesman goes to work. First he warns that a tire is low. Then he goes around to the passenger side of the car to check—out of the driver's sight. Instead of putting air into the tire, he releases a few pounds. After the car is gassed up, the sharpie checks the tire again. He reports a two-pound loss in a matter of minutes. Next, he gets your car into the service bay. Once inside, he uses one of the tools of his trade—a screwdriver sharpened to a needle point, a dart tip, or a special ring he's wearing called a slasher—to poke a hole in the tire. Then when the tire is immersed in water it bubbles, bearing out the salesman's contention that "there is a hole somewhere."

But holes can be patched, so he goes one step further. Inside every tire there is a seam running across the first layer of rubber and fabric. The salesman pushes that part almost inside out to distort the seam as evidence that the tire has had it. He graciously offers to put on the spare. But when he takes the spare to the air hose to fill it up, he slices it with his same well-concealed weapon and then goes through the same routine.

With two tires gone, you have the choice of trying to make it on three tires or buying tires from this helpful station attendant. You buy, of course; testimony from the trial of one of these gyp artists in Los Angeles showed $8000 to $10,000 worth of tires being sold this way in one month. As an added touch of larceny, some salesmen repair the tires they puncture and sell them to the next pigeon who comes in.

The Los Angeles police department's investigation found that tires, batteries, and shock absorbers were the items most often sold by such stations. These shady practices are most likely to occur at service stations that attract tourists. The Los Angeles–Las Vegas run has been a particularly dangerous one for the unsuspicious driver in California, and there is evidence that this form of highway robbery is not confined to the West Coast. The attorneys general offices of Massachusetts and New York have numerous reports of service stations cheating motorists on the popular eastern vacation routes.

Although the big oil companies behind the service stations pretend to be unaware of this highway thievery, they would have to be blind to statistics not to

know that these stations are selling far more accessories than the traffic warrants.

"We were disturbed to learn that the vast majority
of the complaints received [by the attorneys general
of California and Arizona] about fraudulent service
station practices involved the dealerships of major
oil companies," said Elizabeth Hanford, Deputy Director of the White House Office of Consumer Affairs.
"These practices can't be blamed on the fly-by-
nighters," she said.

Ms. Hanford also noted that the state officials reported that even when oil companies were aware of
complaints against their service station operators, the
companies took no action. "One company, for example, had a two-foot-high stack of complaints against
a single dealer, but the standard reply to complaints
was, 'Sorry, there is nothing we can do about our
independent dealers,' " she said.

There are signs that some oil companies are starting
to take a few corrective steps. Mobil Oil Company
and Atlantic-Richfield Company have begun to include consumer protection clauses in some of their
service station leases. Mobil, for example, specifies
that the company may terminate an operator's lease
if it receives a substantial number of consumer complaints about unethical or fraudulent practices.

Such steps are long overdue. But there is still no
reason why oil companies can't keep closer tabs on
their dealers' auto repair activities to prevent motorists
from being defrauded in the first place instead of
merely relying on complaints from consumers who already have been ripped off.

One of the best ways to deter an auto repair gyp
on the highway is to take the name and address of

the salesman who tries to sell you a new tire or battery. If he then seems reluctant, take your business elsewhere.

If you're unfortunate enough to be one of those motorists with only three tires left and have little choice, you may have recourse against the oil company that franchises the station. How that prospect was enhanced by a recent court decision will be described in part five of this book on how to get your money back.

Frauds at Home

Like auto accidents, most auto repair frauds probably occur within twenty-five miles of home. The same motorist who keeps his guard up while traveling, leads with his pocketbook when dealing with his local fix-it shop.

He is likely to run into troubles like those a Washington, D.C. schoolteacher discovered when he went to pick up his Volvo, left at a downtown garage one day for routine repairs. To his shock, he was greeted with a $130 repair bill, including $98 for labor. The "explanation" was 9.8 hours of labor at $10 per hour. Though mystified by the rabbit-up-the-sleeve trick of getting 9.8 hours out of an eight-hour day, the teacher was unable to do anything but pay up and drive off. That's what the mechanic was banking on.

Here are some repair frauds that can, and frequently do, turn up right around home and in the best neighborhoods.

The Expanding Labor Charge

Many repairmen make up for what they consider a low return on some repairs by simply charging for more labor time than it really took to fix your car.

The work order seldom has the labor charge broken down. It usually appears in a lump sum beneath a listing of the repairs performed. Although labor charges are the easiest item to inflate, they are not too difficult to check if the labor charge is known. For example, your work order calls for flushing the radiator and replacing the radiator cap. The garage charges $3 for the part and $10 for labor. To check the labor charge, ask to see the "flat-rate" manual, a book that lists standard work times for specific repairs. Look up winterizing, radiator flush, and replacement of cap. Flat-rate time allotment: .5 hour. Multiply that by the labor charge. If the labor charge per hour is $8, the labor cost of the job should be $4. If there is more than one repair simply add up the time allotted for each repair and multiply by the hourly rate.

When doing business with your dealer, you should expect to be shown the auto manufacturer's flat-rate manual. At an independent garage or gas station, expect to see the Chilton's manual. Chilton's generally allows more time for repairs. Sometimes car dealers try to pay their mechanics by the manufacturer's flat-rate time while charging the customer by Chilton's flat-rate time. Never accept Chilton time from the dealer.

(Flat-rate manuals are explained more fully in part four.)

The Phone Call

Many car owners leave their phone number with the mechanic so that he can call later in the day with an estimate to fix the car. This sets the stage for a midday call from the mechanic to inform the customer that he has discovered some other items that need to be repaired or replaced. The car owner, in his office or at home, is in no position to make an educated decision. He wants his car back and he wants it back soon. The fact that he took the car in to have the windshield wipers adjusted is forgotten. This strategically placed phone call sees to that.

The phony phone estimate is responsible for an enormous amount of repairs charged for that the customer originally did not ask for, probably does not need, and most likely will not get. When on the other end of such a call, you would be wise to get another diagnosis if the repairs are major. This is especially true if the car was taken in for, say, an exhaust leak, and the mechanic calls and recommends a transmission overhaul. It's not likely the mechanic would have gotten anywhere near the transmission in the course of exhaust repairs unless he was looking for trouble —for you.

The Escalating Estimate (*Closely Related to "The Phone Call"*)

With a worried look on your face, you take your car into a repair shop in the morning. "How much will it cost to fix?" you ask the service manager, that smiling personality who greets the anxious driver. Since the service manager is more a salesman than a mechanic, he's rather vague. Without looking under your hood, or into your eyes, he says $75 and writes up a repair order.

Later in the day you get a call from the mechanic who has taken your engine apart. One hundred fifty dollars, he says. You can back out now but it still will cost you $75 to have your engine put back together. You say go ahead. A few hours later you get another call. The mechanic found something else wrong. It will now cost you $240. Of course, if you want to use cheap parts they can do it for $200; but for $240 you will get a guarantee.

The Long Delay

The phone call racket and the escalating estimate are kin to another garage tactic: the long delay. Most drivers depend on their cars for their daily activities. The best way to wear down a driver's reluctance to authorize repairs is to delay. Often, a driver will agree to almost anything to get the car back.

The best advice: don't give in. Whether the ploy being used is the phone call, the escalating estimate, or the long delay, stick to what you went in for and get a written estimate at that time. If the repairs needed, or the estimate, vary widely from your original conversation when you left the garage, take the time to get another opinion. Most times such tactics are a sign the garage is out to pad your bill.

The Phantom Part

Some mechanics keep a stock of old parts handy to pass off as the parts from a cautious shopper's car to show how badly it needs repairs. You might think your engine is cooling adequately, but after the mechanic shows you a fraying fan belt, you are not so sure. Your spark plugs were just changed, but when the mechanic shows you a badly worn plug doubt creeps in. Millions of unneeded parts are sold this way. But many times, the mechanic just puts your own part back while charging for a new part plus labor. Some shops just recycle plugs. The plugs taken out of your car will be cleaned; the next guy who comes in and is convinced he needs new plugs will get yours. And so it goes.

Witnesses at Senator Hart's subcommittee on auto repairs estimated the phantom parts racket costs millions of dollars each year. The best way to protect yourself is to paint or mark your parts.

Nonexistent Services

Many garages, trying to drum up business, advertise "free towing," "free loan car," and "instant credit." Often, there is only one loan car and that's being used, one tow truck and that's being repaired, and instant credit is available at the loan company next door at 20 percent interest. If the services are available, only those who accept and pay for repairs get them free. As a rule of thumb, garages that need to use such advertising to bring in business don't rely on regular customers and tend to be less conscientious than those that do. A study of auto repair in Washington, D.C., made by Ralph Nader's Center for Auto Safety found that of thirty honest, competent shops only two advertised, and they were new-car dealers.

The Board Meeting

You take your car down to the local service station some evening because you think the spark plugs need to be cleaned. Your car goes into the service bay and the hood goes up. The mechanic is about to clean the spark plugs, but diverts his attention to the carburetor. He asks you to start the car. Then he asks one of the gas pump jockeys to peer inside your car. Then he invites the parts salesmen to take a look. Soon they are all gathered around your car, tongues clucking over an ailing engine.

These "board meetings" are scheduled affairs at some garages. Beware of the camaraderie and get another opinion.

The Coat of Paint

There is a practice in the auto repair industry of painting rebuilt parts. Each garage has its own colors. While this penchant for painting is innocent in itself, it means more trouble for car owners. For example, you may be told you need a new starter when all you really need is to have the switch replaced. The garage will fix the switch, slap a coat of paint on the starter, and present you with a bill for a new starter rather than a new switch—a difference of about $60. Generally, you have no way of knowing if this has been done.

If you suspect such a trick, go to another garage and compare your starter to a new one. If the edges on yours look worn down, you have a new coat of paint and little else. This trick applies equally well to automatic transmission repairs where a $10 adjustment to the vacuum modulator, a small part that controls the transmission gears, is parlayed into a transmission "rebuild," thanks to a can of paint.

The best defense against this kind of trickery is to paint a dot or an X on the replaceable parts in your car. Then when you ask to see the old part that has been removed from your car, you'll be able to tell if it's yours.

The Leaders

Almost as old as the automobile, the "leader" comes on as a fantastically low price for an auto repair job such as transmission overhaul, $50; brakes relined, $19.95; front end aligned, $5.95. Advertisements for a $19.95 brake job with a lifetime guarantee lure many a motorist into the garage and his car onto the rack. Once on the rack, the repair on special won't do. Instead of relining the brakes, the mechanic will replace the master cylinder for $80 and toss in a worthless guarantee which covers the cost of replacing the linings. What's more, this flimsy guarantee requires frequent return visits to keep it in effect, giving the shop additional opportunities to sell more repairs.

A Maryland radio announcer, attracted to a brake specialty shop by a low-priced brake special, found his brakes squealing the day after repairs. Instead of going back to the shop that did the job the first time, he went to a second center in the same chain. After he was told a complete brake job was needed and the work was well under way, the announcer produced his fresh guarantee from the first shop. Caught with the company's promises down, the second shop finished the repairs.

In a move against such practices, the Federal Trade Commission charged Market Tire Company of Maryland, Inc., with "lo-balling" customers at its Nationwide Safti-Brake Centers by falsely advertising complete brake relining jobs for as low as $13.95 in order to attract buyers. The customers then were induced to buy additional repairs, the FTC alleged. Officials of Market Tire denied the charges, but they agreed to an FTC consent order prohibiting Nationwide from making deceptive pricing offers.

Follow up these ads only if you are sure the advertised special is the only repair you need and promise yourself that you will get that repair and no other. If the man at the service shop tells you the low-priced repair advertised isn't really as good a bargain as a slightly more expensive job using higher quality and longer wearing materials, take his word for it and consider getting the more realistically priced repair— elsewhere.

The $75 Transmission Overhaul

The transmission gyp usually begins as a "leader," but deserves special mention because it is so widespread and so costly. Automotive engineers agree that the transmission is the most complex component in your car. Consequently, it is most expensive to repair and turns many car owners with broken transmissions into foolhardy bargain hunters. What's facing the bargain hunters is a jungle of "transmission specialists" who promise to fix your transmission for a ridiculously low price but end up handing back your parts in a basket.

In a crackdown on transmission gyp artists, the U.S. attorney's office in Washington, D.C., uncovered a *modus operandi* typical of many crooked shops. It goes like this.

You walk in complaining of transmission trouble, having seen an ad in the paper for a special on transmission repairs. The mechanic may or may not take the car for a road test, which he will ignore anyway. He wants to get your car up on the rack. He'll usually accomplish this by telling you that a road test isn't enough, that he has to look inside the transmission to diagnose the problem. He then takes the transmission apart. The diagnosis varies but the price is usually the same—$200 or $300. The advertised special is never adequate.

By this time, you may decide the price is a bit much and maybe this shop isn't all its advertisement cracked it up to be. You tell the mechanic you want to go get another estimate. He tells you that will be $75 or he will leave your transmission scattered in so many pieces around the shop. At that point, you have been taken for at least $75. The U.S. attorney's records indicate that many car owners are taken for the whole bundle by deciding to go ahead and have the repairs made there. And, in many of these cases, no work will be done on the transmission. The mechanic will make the needed adjustment, repaint your transmission and clear several hundred dollars on the job.

In other cases, the fraud is more subtle. You leave

your car for transmission repairs. The mechanic replaces the vacuum modulator which costs $20, but charges you $300 for a rebuilt transmission. Or he adjusts the transmission's rings and bands, calls it a transmission overhaul and charges $200.

There are ways to avoid transmission gyps. First, don't let anyone take your transmission apart until you are absolutely certain the problem is inside. Automotive engineers estimate that 80 percent of all transmission problems can be diagnosed and fixed without taking the unit apart. If the shop you are at can't find the problem without dismantling the transmission, give a few other places a crack at it.

Second, avoid places with flashy ads for transmission overhauls and rebuilt transmissions. Most good transmission shops don't advertise much because they don't have to.

Third, turn to chapter 7 in this book on common trouble signs and look under transmissions for the list of items to check before diagnosing the trouble as "in the transmission."

Fourth, if the problem is the transmission, there are several repairs that can be made that do not require dismantling the unit. Eliminate those repairs as the possible answer before moving on to the more expensive repairs inside.

part two ————————————————

How to Tell What Repairs Are Needed

What to Do When Your Car Won't Start

Everyone knows the sinking sensation that comes when the car won't start or when it stops in midstream.

The American Automobile Association answers approximately 10 million such sinking calls per year. The reason for the call in the overwhelming number of cases is battery and electrical trouble.

Since most people don't belong to AAA, a short primer on how to track down battery and electrical problems, as well as some others, is included here in hopes you may be able to avoid an expensive towing bill by making a temporary fix yourself. Some tow trucks have instructions not to start an ailing auto but to tow it back to the garage where the "experts" can decide how much to take you for.

Just remember that the fix probably is only temporary and permanent repairs may be needed.

Things to Try

Depending upon your temperament, you may want to try only one or two items before calling the tow truck. What is included here is a list of things a non-mechanic would be able to do. How far you will get into the list will depend on how hot, or tired, or hungry you are when you break down. On a good day, you might try them all.

—Turn on your lights. If they are bright, you have a good battery and should skip the next three steps.

—Check the battery terminals for corrosion. Corrosion is caused by acid boiled out of the battery, white to bluish green. Take a sharp instrument and knock off the deposit and then wipe with an old rag. Use an old one because it will dissolve from the acid. Do the same thing to the cables. If you remove the cables, be sure to remove the *negative* cable first, otherwise the alternator can be ruined and the battery destroyed. The negative cable is always the smaller of the two cables. When putting the cables back, always hook the *positive* cable on first.

Now try to start the car. If it works, you are on your way after losing about five minutes time.

—If that didn't work, check the water inside the battery. It should be filled to about three quarters of an inch below the top. Check all six cells. Most General Motors cars have an "eye" for checking the level of the solution. There is only one and so you can only check one cell, instead of all six, and it often gets discolored. To be safe, make a visual check of all six cells. If the solution is low, add water to the fill line inside the battery (usually three quarters of an inch from the top). If the car then starts, make sure you run it for at least a half hour to get the charge back up.

—If you have a manual shift car, you can skip the above and run the car on the generator or alternator. Put the car in third, point it down a hill if there is one handy, or get a push if not, then let out the clutch and press down on the accelerator when you get going a bit. Never try to push-start automatics, but use jumper cables hooked up to the battery of a friendly car. Never start either car until the cables are attached. Make sure you attach one cable to the positive terminals of both batteries and the other to the negative terminals. The terminals are marked with a plus sign for positive and a minus sign for negative.

If instead of even a brief straining sound you get just a click when you try to start the car, the problem is probably not the battery but somewhere in the starter system.

—A simple thing that goes wrong in many cars, especially Chevrolets, is that the plug of about five wires that connects the key switch to the ignition switch comes loose. To fix, reach behind the key and push the plug of wires back in the hole. It's like plugging an iron in a socket at home. Since the wires contain only twelve volts, you can't get a shock. (Electric toy trains contain twice as many volts.) If the switch catches, you are on your way with no serious problems. Even if the switch isn't out of the hole, give it a good push. The connections may be loose.

—In manual shift cars, the click could mean the starter is hung up in the flywheel. What you can do to get going is put the car in third gear and push backward. This will unlock the starter assembly and the fan belt should start turning again. Permanent fix: tighten the starter bolts.

Other battery, starter, and electrical checks are omitted. They are more complicated than those described here and would entail more tools and mechanical knowledge than you would want to get into.

Other easy checks outside the electrical system:

—The fan belt. It's easy to spot because it is just in front of the engine and looks a lot like a belt. If it is broken, some mechanics say you can improvise for a short period with a belt without a buckle. Put it around the pulleys where the fan belt was.

If the belt is not broken but deflects more than one half to three quarters of an inch when you push on it, it's too loose to do its job well. With a loose belt you can wait for the engine to cool and go a few miles and get a new belt. On the other hand, one of the pulleys may be broken, in which case you need a larger repair.

If there is a nearby service area and the fan belt is out of commission, you can run the car for a few minutes, stop for fifteen, and then run it again. If you haven't got the time for that, you may have to call a tow truck because driving without a fan belt can overheat the engine and do a lot of permanent damage.

—If the weather is hot and the engine is hot, you may just have vapor lock. Raise the hood and let the engine cool. You can speed the cooling by placing ice around the fuel line and fuel pump, or just pour cold water on the whole thing. If you have neither water nor ice, take a fifteen-minute rest stop. In any case, never remove the radiator cap when the engine is hot. This makes the inside solution boil out and over, causing damage to other parts of the car and to anyone in the area.

If the engine cranks but just won't quite turn over, you should check the fuel system. Starting with the easiest solutions, here's what to try:

—If you smell gasoline, you may have flooded the carburetor trying to start the car. Press the accelerator

to the floor, wait a few moments, and then turn the
key. This will open the choke a little extra to allow
more air to mix with the gas overflow.

—Remove the air cleaner and filter from atop the
carburetor. The filter may be clogged and keeping air
from mixing with the gas. Try to start the car again.

—Pull off the distributor cap and wipe off the inside with a rag. If it has a crack, you need a new one.
If it just had dirt deposits, wiping it off may get you
going again.

—With the air cleaner still off, take the plastic
handle of a screwdriver or a hairbrush, or something
of similar weight, and give the carburetor a few sharp
knocks. Not only will this relieve some frustration,
but in a surprising number of cases it loosens up dirt
or carbon deposits which are keeping a needle inside
the carburetor from going up and down like it is supposed to, and gets the car going again. But banging
will work only for a while. Take this as a sign your
carburetor needs cleaning.

—Stick the screwdriver, or a twig or something,
down in the carburetor to open the choke plate while
someone else starts the car. (It is better to break down
with a friend.) If there is only one of you, push open
the choke plate so it looks like it might stay and then
crank the engine. This should get air to the gas if the
choke is stuck closed. (If the engine is cold, the choke
may be stuck open too much and you may have to
push it shut.)

—If that didn't work, and you still have that friend,
one of you press the accelerator while the other listens
over the carburetor to hear if the gas is spraying inside. If you're alone, find the metal lever next to the
carburetor that moves when you press the accelerator

pedal and move it. If there is no gas spraying inside, you have water or something in there.

If so, make a tent with your hands over the neck of the carburetor, preferably while someone else starts the car. If you're still alone, and have long arms, cup one hand over the carburetor neck and crank the engine with your free hand. The resulting suction should clear out the carburetor temporarily and get the gas flowing in the right direction. For a permanent fix, you need a carburetor cleaning.

If the easy things didn't work, and you still have the energy, there are a few last checks before calling for the tow truck.

—Check the various hoses and pumps that get the fuel to your engine to see if maybe they are clogged. As noted in the section on fuel systems, you can loosen the strawlike gas line between the carburetor and the fuel pump and clear it out with a pipe cleaner or by blowing into it. And you can take the cap off the top of the fuel pump, clean it out, press the accelerator a few times to get gas into the lines and then try to start the car.

—Finally, you can try one last trick in the electrical system. Take off the distributor cap. Right in front of you will be the points. If they look burned, dirty, or pitted, they are not able to do their job to start your car. You can clean them temporarily with the striking surface of a matchbook cover, or a nail file. This should get you going in an emergency. But get new points.

Miscellaneous Problems

—If you have been driving through deep water and the car stalls, press the accelerator to the floor to clear the engine. Wait a few moments and then try to start. If this fails, lift the hood, pull the boots off the spark plugs, dry off the boots and the ends of the spark plugs (the white porcelain part). If the problem is wet spark plugs and you have patience, just wait fifteen minutes and let the heat from the engine dry them.

—Sometimes the car will turn over, start, and idle, but won't accelerate. In this case, check to see that the cable that goes from the floor pedal accelerator to the carburetor is attached. It may be hanging free or have come loose from its clamp. If it has, look for the clamp, which will probably be lying somewhere inside the engine compartment. Put the clamp back on the lever next to the carburetor, attach the cable to it, and when you press the accelerator pedal, the lever, and your car, should respond.

Often the starting problem occurs in the morning when you first try to get the car going. A panel of service experts have this advice for when the engine won't turn over or it gets flooded:

In cold weather: Before turning the ignition, press the accelerator to the floor four times. Then turn the car on and press the accelerator a quarter of the way down. Car should start the first try.

In mild weather: Press accelerator to the floor twice, then hold a quarter of the way down to start.

In hot weather: Just press the pedal to the floor

once, then turn the key and start with the accelerator a quarter of the way down.

In wet weather: Ignition wires simply may be wet. Wipe them off with a rag, or spray them with a moisture-removing spray sold in auto accessory shops.

chapter 4 ─────────────────────

Auto Repair Courses

If you really don't know a carburetor from a distributor cap and want to learn, help is on the way. Alarmed by the rise in blue-collar crime, government and private organizations are offering consumer protection courses hoping to educate the citizenry to the ways they can be cheated. The most popular course is auto repair. Courses are springing up in many cities under the auspices of universities, community colleges, the adult education programs of local high schools, and the YMCAs. In some cities, the Independent Garage Owners of America are offering classes.

Car repair classes don't try to make mechanics out of the students. They just hope to change car owners from easy marks into knowledgeable consumers. Most students who enroll are not interested in crawling under their autos with a kit full of tools. They simply want to know how a car runs, some basic trouble-shooting techniques, and how much repairs should cost.

Most students never perform an engine tune-up. But they do learn that many times what's needed is not a tune-up but a carburetor adjustment or a new PCV * valve, an antipollution device.

* Positive Crankcase Ventilation.

Learning the vocabulary, techniques, and economics of the auto repair industry takes time—usually the classes meet once a week for several months. But those few hours can save you a bundle. A mechanic puts your car up on the rack and shows you a loose, wobbly wheel. He confides that your auto needs front-end repairs costing upward of $100. If you have attended an auto repair course, you know that a wheel with no weight on it always wobbles and nothing is wrong with the front end.

Women have even more opportunities than men to enroll in auto repair classes. Recognizing that many women are in charge of the family car and generally are more vulnerable to auto repair sharks, a number of women's clubs and civic organizations are bringing in mechanics to teach the difference between a spark plug and a shock absorber.

When a mechanic tried to tell Mrs. Rosemary Smith of Camp Hill, Pennsylvania, that the black grime on the end of her car's spark plug meant a rebuilt engine was needed, he didn't know that the local Camp Hill Civic Club had had one of his colleagues teaching the nuts and bolts of auto repairs for the past month. Mrs. Smith was a pupil and had learned her lessons well. She told the mechanic to adjust the carburetor—the black deposit at the tip of a spark plug indicates too rich a fuel mixture. Her attentiveness during class saved her at least $100.

The number of community colleges and adult education departments offering car repair courses for the consumer has grown so tremendously that it is impossible to list them all. For further information, write to the Office of Vocational Education, Department of Health, Education and Welfare, Washington, D.C.

Another source of information is the President's Office of Consumer Affairs, Consumer Education Division, 17th and Pennsylvania Avenues, Washington, D.C.

The quickest way to find out what is offered in your area is to look under your county or city government listing for adult education. If you have a community college in your area, chances are they sponsor an evening auto repair course. Northern Virginia Community College, which has both a consumer course in auto repair and one for aspiring mechanics, has an added bonus: They will take your car and fix it for you.

The Diagnostic Center

Sooner or later, you're going to have to rely on professional help to make the final diagnosis and repair of your car's troubles. For major repairs, don't settle for just the first verdict that comes along. Shop around for one or two estimates on what's needed and how much it should cost, just as you would comparison shop for other major purchases. Automobiles are almost as complicated as people and even the most honest mechanic can mistake a minor ailment for a major one.

At this point, you might want to consider running your car through one of those computerized, diagnostic centers to pinpoint needed repairs. If so, approach with extreme caution. Back in the early 1960s, diagnostic centers were hailed as the panacea for all the car owner's problems. But as it has worked out, the fancy equipment often is used more as a marketing tool for unneeded repairs than an honest, objective appraisal of what your car needs.

Diagnostic centers, in effect, put your car under an electronic stethoscope and elaborate testing to diagnose all its ailments. Once the tests are completed, a friendly technician, much like the family doctor, sits down with you and the test results to discuss what major operations are needed. The diagnosis generally costs from $8 to $15.

Investors in diagnostic equipment, however, quickly discovered how expensive it is to operate, and just as quickly they opened up repair shops next door— hoping to make up in repairs what they were spending on machines. Garagemen, aware of their poor public image, latched on to the idea as an easy way to prove they were good guys and sell repairs at the same time —if the machine says you need the repairs, you must need them.

But a machine, no matter how expensive, is only as honest or as good as the man running it. A mechanic, anxious to pad your bill with unneeded repairs, can do it even more easily with a dynamometer at his side.

For instance, the Center for Auto Safety took a 1966 Plymouth Valiant to Call Carl, a large auto repair chain in Washington, D.C., to be run through their diagnostic equipment. The diagnosis: $140 in repairs to put the car back in good shape. On the same day, the same car was taken to Market Tire's diagnostic center, which failed another system of the car. Estimate for repairs: $206. Both diagnostic centers perform repairs. The diagnosis of a trusted mechanic showed that at most a brake job was needed— neither diagnostic center failed the brakes—at a cost of $70 or $80.

A 1965 Dodge was taken to an independently run diagnostic center in Denver, Colorado, which uncovered eleven faults, most of which could be fixed by simple adjustments. The car was then taken to a diagnostic center that was part of a garage. Diagnosis: a very sick engine. Cost of repairs: $275.

Some attribute the differing diagnoses to the human element. Critics see the lure of high repair bills as too great for many diagnostic centers to use their equipment just for diagnosis. It's much more valuable as a repair salesman.

Whatever the reason, diagnostic centers haven't lived up to their advance billing as an impartial answer to the car owner's repair woes. It's not that a diagnostic center is automatically untrustworthy because it also sells repairs. Some operations can wear their diagnostic and repair hats independently and honestly. It's just that the average motorist has no way of telling the white hats from the black hats.

The evidence thus far indicates you'd best be wary about counting on diagnostic repair shops for unbiased opinions about your car's condition. However, if past experience indicates your local shop is a straight shooter, a diagnostic check might be a good way to spot current and future problems. Diagnostic centers also can be useful in situations where there is no reason for the garage to think you will turn your car over for repair. For instance, you can find out the truth about that shiny used, or even new, car you're eyeing. No garage expects you to buy repairs for a car that isn't yours.

—Just before your new-car warranty expires, you can get a complete diagnosis of your car's ills. Most diagnostic centers understand the logic in finding out what's wrong before you have to foot the bill.

—When you have a badly ailing car that might better be relegated to the junk heap or traded in than repaired, diagnostic analysis can be useful. Explain to the technician that you have no intention of repairing the vehicle but are only interested in its trade-in or scrap value.

Potentially, diagnostic centers can offer some salvation to motorists if the diagnosis can be divorced from repairs. If Senator Philip Hart has his way, a network of independent diagnostic centers will be set up across the country. Here, for several dollars, you will be able to have your car diagnosed and find out what repairs are needed. After you have the repairs made elsewhere, you can return to see just how well the job was performed.

Only a few independent diagnostic centers exist at the moment. They are included here for those fortunate enough to live in cities where they are located. There is a movement afoot among the nation's auto clubs to provide independent diagnosis for their members. Check with your local AAA to find out if they have this service.

Independent Diagnostic Centers—Not Associated with a Repair Garage

Auto Analysts, Sacramento, California
Auto Analysts, Denver, Colorado
Farrar Brown Car Check, Biddeford, Maine
Nelson Safety, Minneapolis, Minnesota
Somerset Auto Diagnosis, Somerville, New Jersey
Bear Manufacturers, Rock Island, Illinois
Riverside Auto Lab, Riverside, California
Electro-Chek Auto Diagnostic Center, Seattle, Washington

Auto Clubs Offering Independent Diagnosis
California State Auto Association Clubs
150 Van Ness Avenue
San Francisco, California 94102

St. Louis, Missouri Auto Club
3917 Lindell Boulevard
St. Louis, Missouri 63108

San Jose Auto Club
Cardoc Diagnosis Center
La Mesa, California 92041

Is the Repair Worth Making,
or Has Your Car Had It?

It is cheaper to own an old car than it is to own a new car, according to every study made on the cost of automobile upkeep. You lose money the first two years you own a new car. After that, the auto begins to pay you back in terms of what you can sell it for and how much it costs you to keep it running.

Detroit auto makers will tell you it is best to trade in your car every two or three years because that's when repair costs start mounting. What they don't tell you is that it's best for them, not you. The higher repair expenses on a two- or three-year-old car don't come close to matching the depreciation cost alone on a new car.

A study published by the U.S. Department of Transportation illustrates the economics of old versus new car ownership. (Tables of the estimated cost of operating a car from the first year of ownership to the tenth will be found in appendix 1.)

A popular four-door sedan (1972 model) costs about $4379 to buy new. This includes power steering, V-8 engine, an automatic transmission, and all taxes. By the time the car completes a ten-year, 100,000-mile journey from the new-car lot to the junkyard, its operating cost will total $13,552.95. This averages out to a cost of nearly 14 cents a mile over the ten years. The study assumes the car will be driven fewer miles each year, ranging from 14,500 miles the first year to 5700 the tenth year.

(The government study shows that the operating costs are less for compact and subcompact cars, but the pattern of the expenses is pretty much the same.)

The most expensive of these ten years is the first, when depreciation cost is the greatest single expense at 8.5 cents a mile. Depreciation continues to be the biggest cost until the car is five years old, but eventually declines to 0.8 cents per mile by the tenth year. The new car in the Transportation Department study depreciates $1226 the first year, $900 the second, $675 the third and less each year afterwards until that item totals only $48 in the tenth year.

Repairs do start increasing in the car's third year when the mileage averages between 27,000 and 39,000 miles. But the repair and maintenance cost in the third year still is only 2.1 cents a mile, more than 6 cents less per mile than depreciation alone on a new car in its first year. And the overall operating cost dips to 13.3 cents a mile from 13.8 cents the first year, including gasoline, oil, insurance, parking, taxes, and license fees. Based on a third-year mileage of 11,500 miles, that's a one-year savings of $469.32 for your three-year-old car over your neighbor's shiny new model.

By the time the car is five years and nearly 60,000 miles old, the operating cost drops to 12.4 cents per mile; and by the time it is chugging through its ninth and tenth years the cost is down to a low of between 9 cents and 11 cents per mile.

Actually, the economy of an older car is even greater because the Transportation Department study doesn't take into account the high cost of financing a new car—an item that can add several pennies to the cost of every mile. This "could easily amount to more than $100 a year for the person who customarily trades in his car so that he always owns the 'latest models,' " estimates the department.

Of course, there are other factors besides economy which must be taken into consideration when deciding whether to keep that old car. Comfort and appearance are of primary importance to some people. Although recent trends in auto sales indicate that buyers are becoming more interested in substance than style, there still seems to be a public willingness to pay through the nose for annual styling changes and expensive gimmicks like concealed headlights, tinted windshields, and hidden radio antennas. When these factors are added in, the five-year-old car, despite its economy, becomes less desirable.

If appearance and newness are paramount, you probably want to put your money into a new model instead of buying replacement parts for your "old" car. Repair costs start mounting after a car's second year, or at about 25,000 to 30,000 miles. If you must, that probably is about the best time to get back on the treadmill of high depreciation and still more "easy monthly payments." But it still is much more expensive to buy a new car than to keep the old one repaired.

The crucial time for deciding whether to pour more money into the old car or to put it toward a new, and perhaps more reliable, one comes at about 60,000 miles. The Transportation Department study shows that it is between 60,000 and 70,000 miles that repair bills hit their peaks, rising to 4.2 cents a mile after 69,000 miles.

It is at this point that really major repairs are likely to be needed. The government cost study, for example, includes a valve job costing more than $100 at the 70,000-mile mark. If you're ready to move up to a newer car, or indications are the repairs needed on your old one may be more extensive than usual, now might be the time to bail out.

(For what it's worth, the federal government's standard for replacing cars at government agencies is six years or 60,000 miles.)

But if all you care about is economy, it's still cheaper to keep the old clunker. Despite the jump in repair outlays, the overall cost of 12 cents a mile for the government's hypothetical study car in its seventh year is still below the 13.7 cents for a new car.

Statistics, however, always talk about averages and your situation might warrant a different decision. For those who distrust statistics, there are other tests for assessing whether your car is worth keeping.

Body rust, sometimes indicative of deterioration of vital automobile components, is one consideration. Another, the condition of your engine. Parts do wear out, some faster than others, inside the engine. Does your engine need several new parts or will it need a rebuild soon? Are the springs out of the seats and the interior upholstery falling apart? Is the front end just out of line or do you need new universal joints, ball joints, shocks?

The following questionnaire published by *Better Homes and Gardens* magazine might help you determine if your car is worth saving. If you come out 85 or better, it would probably be to your advantage to keep the car for a while. Between 50 and 84, it's a borderline case and you will have to evaluate how important having a new model is to you. Below 50, the car may be costing you more than it's worth.

	POOR	FAIR	GOOD	EXCEL-LENT
Body exterior (dents, rust, chrome, paint)	0	5	15	25
Body interior (upholstery, headliner, instrument panel, carpeting)	0	5	12	20
Engine (noise, oil consumption, poor performance)	1	4	12	18
Drive train (transmission, rear end—leaks, klunks, slippage)	2	5	10	15
Cooling system (radiator, hose, thermostat, water pump, heater core)	2	4	5	7
Electrical system (alternator, starter, battery)	3	4	6	8
Suspension and steering (worn parts, alignment, springs, shocks)	2	5	8	12
Tires—tread depth (*excellent:* 10/32–11/32 in.; *good:* 6/32–9/32 in.; *fair:* 3/32–5/32 in.; *poor:* 2/32 in. and under)	2	3	5	7
Exhaust system (exhaust pipe, muffler(s), tail pipe)	2	3	5	7
Brakes (how long since major overhaul? stop straight and dependably?)	2	4	6	9
Miscellaneous (accessories, heater, air conditioner, etc. in working order?)	2	3	4	5

NOTE: Reprinted, by permission, from "How to Know When Your Car Has Had It," *Better Homes and Gardens* (July 1970). © Meredith Corporation, 1970.

Common Trouble Signs

The best defense against unneeded repairs is a little self-diagnosis before taking your car into the fix-it shop. The more you can learn about how your car works, the better off you'll be. But you don't have to be an amateur mechanic to get an idea of what may be wrong. You do need to know how to spot some of the common warning signs and know what they mean. Even if you're not sure what repairs are needed, just sounding knowledgeable enough so that the mechanic *thinks* you do can be half the battle.

Many mechanics admit that a little knowledge on the part of the customer can go a long way. "I'm not against making a few extra dollars on a slow day. But if a customer comes in and has an idea of what's wrong with his car, he cuts my diagnosis time in half, and we both make out better," says one New York City repairman who does $500,000 worth of business annually. "Besides," he concedes, "I don't want to take a chance of cheating a guy who might know what's happening."

How Your Car Works

There is no need to get bogged down in technical jargon and mechanical terms, but you should have at least a basic idea of how your car runs. The following is a brief—and, hopefully, painless—description.

To get the whole process under way you need electricity. Turning the key in the ignition switch sets off a flow of electricity supplied by the energy stored in your car's battery. The electricity flows first through the points and coil, a transformer which steps up the electric current and sends it on to the distributor. The distributor, which resembles a bunch of fingers, separates the flow and parcels it out through its fingers

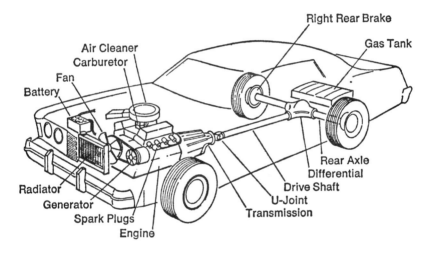

Main parts of a car

(one for each spark plug, usually six or eight depending on the number of cylinders) to arrive at each spark plug in sequence at a precise moment. This causes electrical sparks to jump from the plugs— which is why they are called spark plugs.

Meanwhile, the gasoline in your car is on the move, too. The fuel pump is pumping the gas forward through gas lines from the gas tank in the rear to the carburetor in the front on top of the engine. The carburetor, your car's atomizer, mixes the gasoline with air filtered in through the air filter to form a gasoline vapor. The vapor is sucked in through the intake manifold to the cylinders, the hollow chambers of your engine beneath the spark plugs.

All of this takes place in the fraction of a second after you've turned the key. If all is well, when the electricity meets the atomized gasoline, your car will start. What happens is that the sparks from the spark plugs ignite the gas vapor in the cylinders causing miniature explosions which force the pistons (one inside each cylinder) to move down and up in sequence. Now your car's engine is running and the continuing explosions will help to keep it running.

The up and down movement of the pistons rotates a crankshaft, a bar running through the engine that transfers the power from the pistons to your car's transmission. To get the car moving, you shift gears inside the transmission to spin the power through a long tube called the drive shaft to the rear-end mechanism and the rear axles. The wheels attached to the axles turn and the car moves.

When you want to stop, you push down on your brake pedal to begin another chain reaction that starts with brake fluid being forced out of a "master" cylinder and through tubelike brake lines to brake cylinders at each wheel. The fluid causes small pistons at each end of the cylinders to press against the brake shoes and the shoes' linings which in turn rub against the spinning brake drums to stop the wheels. (With disc brakes, a plierslike device pinches a spinning metal disc on each wheel.)

The burning gasoline and rotating parts create a lot of heat. So a cooling system circulates air and water through the engine to keep it from blowing its cool. This system includes the radiator, the fan, the fan belt, and the water pump. Some cars, like the Volkswagen, use only air to cool the engine.

Lubricating oil from the crankcase keeps all those rotating parts from grinding each other to pieces. And your car's exhaust system—including the muffler and tailpipe—cools the hot escaping gases, deadens their noise, and prevents their deadly fumes from getting inside your car.

Naturally, the workings of a modern automobile are much more complex, but that should give you an idea of what's happening. Now you are ready for some of the common clues to what may be ailing your car and what's needed to fix them. If some of the auto parts terms are too technical, check the glossary in the back of this book to find out what they mean.

Leaks and What They Mean

Everyone can identify that blotch under the car as a leak, but few can interpret what it means. If you can distinguish colors, you can decipher what your car is trying to tell you:

Reddish spots: Evaporate quickly. Probably gas.

Oil puddle under the car: Means a bad diaphragm in the fuel pump, a leaky gasket on the crankcase, or a loose oil-pan plug.

Dark blackish, thick substance under the rear axle: Could mean a faulty differential seal.

Pink oil: If under the front of the engine it means

the power steering fluid is leaking. If under the rear of the engine, under the center hump, it's probably transmission fluid, especially if it has a strong smell.

Pale stains: Probably water. A puddle under the radiator means a leak in the radiator or an overheated engine.

Thin clear fluid under the rear of the engine or under any of the wheels: Denotes leaking brake fluid, calling for a further investigation of the brake lines, wheels, and master cylinders.

What Your Exhaust Can Tell You

Smoke from the tailpipe: White smoke indicates a water leak, probably from condensation or a loose gasket. Black smoke may be gasoline; check the fuel system. Bluish gray smoke means an oil leak.

Sounds and What They Mean

If you listen to your car carefully, you may find it is telling you what's wrong. For instance:

Your car makes a rapid hammering sound: This indicates a loose rod or crankshaft bearing, or not enough oil or water. Stop immediately to avoid damage to the engine.

Your car pings like marbles dropped into a coffee can: Possible pre-ignition or spark knock. Indicates bad timing, or carbon deposits. This is a simple repair.

Your car makes a loud slapping sound: This goes along with oil burning and is caused by excessive wear between the pistons and rings. Repair immediately.

Your car squeals on braking: Brakes may need re-lining. If just when you turn the steering wheel all the way left or right, check the steering belt. (Disc brakes may squeal normally.)

Your car clunks: Worn universal joint. Lubricate first. If that doesn't work, replace.

Your car clicks: Could indicate a sticking valve lifter and a costly valve job. But first try using a high-detergent oil.

Your car makes a high-pitched noise, sounding somewhat like you have a chirping bird under the hood: The water pump may be ready to go. Have it checked before you find yourself stalled on the road with an overheated car.

Your car makes a high, whining noise: May be a loose or worn fan belt.

Your car makes a rumbling sound: Hole in the muffler is the likely cause. Also could be a bad rear wheel bearing.

What Your Battery Can Tell You

Most people expect no more than two or three years from a battery. Actually, a battery should last at least 40,000 miles or more. Batteries are a fast-moving item and often an overzealous garage will sell you a new one when cleaning the terminals on the old one, or adding water, would do.

When the fluid level in the battery is down, you may have starting problems. To check the fluid, take off the battery caps, peer inside and see if the water is up to the circle. If not, add water. Although some mechanics say distilled water is better, most now believe regular tap water is just as good. Run the car for a half hour to recharge.

Once or twice a year corrosion on the battery terminals should be scraped off. A car will not start if the deposit on the battery posts and connectors is too thick. After the connectors and battery posts are clean, apply a thin film of petroleum jelly or one of the commercial sprays to prevent further deposits. What you are scraping off the battery is acid. The acid will eat through the rag you use to clean it, and even your clothes and fingers if they get in the way. Baking soda is good for stubborn corrosion. Mix four tablespoons in a glass of water. But be sure no solution gets inside the battery.

Sometimes the corrosion is left too long and gets inside the battery's positive cable. If it does, do not replace the whole cable and cable end as the mechanic will advise. The cables are long and therefore expensive, especially in Buicks and Chevrolets, so replace only the cable end rather than the entire cable. The ends are made of either lead or brass. Lead is much better.

Car owners frequently think their battery is worn out when it is only run down. A battery industry survey showed that one out of every ten batteries replaced was still good—it just needed recharging.

You can check the battery charge yourself with a syringe-type device called a hydrometer, which sells for a couple of dollars at auto supply stores. Simply insert the tube into each battery cell and suck up some fluid; a floating marker measures how much the cell is, or isn't, charging. (With some similar devices you measure by following the floating plastic balls to see if they rise to the top of the tube.)

Or you can have your service station check the battery using its hydrometer.

A service station can also test your battery with a machine that tells you if the battery can be recharged. You can interpret the test yourself—the meter readings usually are marked "good," "defective," or "needs charge." One warning: these machines aren't foolproof, and in the hands of a sharp salesman can be used to convince you to buy a new battery. Before buying a new one (and gas stations aren't the best places to buy batteries anyway), have your battery checked at another station.

What Your Spark Plugs Can Tell You

If your car is hard to start, running roughly, or lacks power, the problem could be in your spark plugs. Then again, it could involve some other part. So before you run out and buy a whole new set of spark plugs or pay for a tune-up, take the time to peek at your plugs.

Spark plugs can be removed with a special spark plug wrench or ratchet. A careful look at the firing ends can tell you a lot about the condition of your engine:

Light brown, dry deposit: Normal appearance. No corrosion.

Dry, black carbon deposits: If on all plugs, the gas mixture is too rich and indicates a carburetor problem, a faulty automatic choke, or a clogged air cleaner. If the dry, black deposit appears at the end of only one plug, you may have a bad spark plug wire on that cylinder; the result is unburned gasoline because there

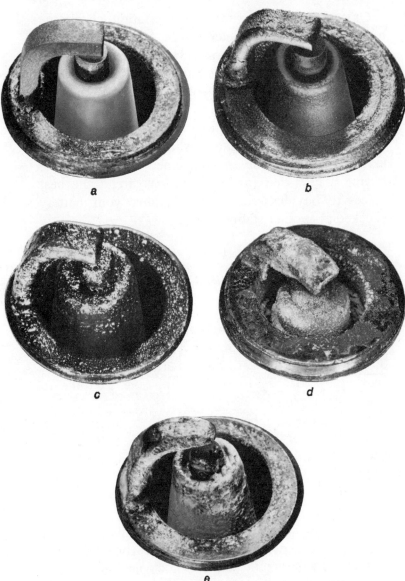

What your spark plugs can tell you: a) Normal appearance—light brown, dry deposit; b) dry, black carbon deposits; c) black, oily, wet deposit; d) white or yellow deposit; e) white blistered end. (Courtesy Champion Spark Plugs, Inc.)

is not enough voltage to fire the gas-air mixture properly.

Black, oily, wet deposit: This is the worst sign. It indicates liquid oil is getting in around the pistons and you may need an overhaul of worn rings or pistons.

White or yellow deposit: This is normal with fuels designed to change the chemical nature of the deposits in order to lessen the plug's tendency to misfire. The deposit is flaky and easily scraped off.

White blistered end: Engine is too hot. You may have spark plugs whose heat range is too high for your engine. If the heat range is too high, the plug ends will burn. If the heat range is right, the white blistered ends may be due to low-octane fuel, inefficient cooling, or bad ignition timing. Sustained high-speed, heavy-load driving can produce high temperatures which require the use of colder spark plugs.

Spark plugs frequently are changed when there is no need for it. No matter what is wrong with your car, some repairman will lift the hood, listen intently, and then tell you to turn off the motor. Then he will remove a perfectly good spark plug and announce that it is burned out.

If you go to the front of the car to see for yourself —and most people don't—you still may not be saved. A sharp mechanic's hand is quicker than the average motorist's eye. Before you can peer over his shoulder, he will bend the plug's center electrode out of shape. "Look," he will say, "there is supposed to be a gap in there. You don't have one." And you will "need" a whole new set of plugs.

By knowing what's wrong with that scenario, you can keep it from playing in your neighborhood theater of car repairs. First, the repairman did not try to find

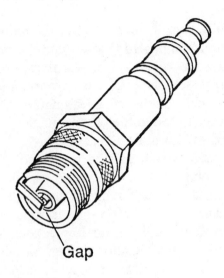

Spark plug, showing gap

which plug wasn't firing by holding the end of each one to see if it was taking a spark from the distributor. Second, spark plugs can be regapped; that is, even if the distance between the outside electrode and the center electrode is off, it is often a simple matter to adjust the gap. Third, all the plugs don't collapse at the same time.

Although it is seldom necessary, mechanics often will replace all the spark plugs rather than just those that are worn out. When only one or two plugs do need replacement, clean the others and put them back for several thousand more miles. After all, you don't replace all four tires when only one wears out. (Some mechanics charge just as much to clean your spark plugs as to replace them. If that's the case you might as well get all eight replaced.)

Spark plug makers suggest replacing plugs every 10,000 miles. Independent mechanics and engineers suggest 12,000 to 15,000 miles between spark plug changes.

Whether you take time to check your spark plugs or not, don't rush to the conclusion that you need a tune-up—which involves replacing the plugs and points—if your car is running sluggishly or stalling, especially if you have less than 10,000 miles on the plugs. The problem could be as simple—and cheap to repair—as a clogged air filter, PCV valve, or some part of your fuel system.

What Your Brakes Can Tell You

When your car won't start, it is always frustrating. But when your car won't stop, it can be deadly.

Fortunately, your brakes send out signals when things begin to go amiss so you can get repairs before reaching the danger point. It is best to follow a strict regimen with brakes. Regular checks can tell you whether the brake fluid and linings are doing their jobs. Inexpensive brake checks are normally needed about every 12,000 miles.

Here's what to look for:

Low brake pedal that must be pumped to stop: Indicates the need for adjustment but not necessarily new linings.

Squealing sound: Usually means the linings have worn down to the rivets and require replacement.

Chatter: Occurs when there is uneven wear or the lining is glazed. If linings are glazed but in good condition otherwise, you can restore their effectiveness by having the surfaces sanded with a medium grade sandpaper.

Brake fade: Indicates badly worn or glazed linings.

Spongy pedal: Means air in the hydraulic system. Bleed the system, which should make the pedal firm again. It also may mean too much clearance between the lining and the drum. Adjust brake shoes.

Mush brake when the car is standing still: If you push the brake pedal down and it feels soft and sinks to the floor, you may have a leaking wheel cylinder or a leaky master brake cylinder. Look for telltale trace of fluid around the tire or drum. Fix leak or replace cylinder.

Dragging brakes: Could indicate the brake shoe return springs are worn out. New ones cost under $10.

Grabbing brakes which are too sensitive to light pressure: Means the linings may be grease soaked. Replace linings.

Hard brake: Usually caused by the normal wear of the brake lining. Make minor brake adjustment to compensate for lining wear.

Car pulls to one side: First check tires for uneven pressure. Then check for grease on the linings and correct by replacing the linings. Otherwise, uneven pressure on the wheels can usually be corrected by an adjustment to the brake shoes.

Excessive pedal travel: Leaks in a cylinder's seal or low fluid in the master cylinder. You should have the mechanic check for leaks and bring fluid up to proper level. Grease seals can be replaced for a few dollars per wheel. (*Warning:* Don't take chances with a leaking master cylinder. Nothing is more dangerous.)

Brakes will not hold in wet weather: If brakes suddenly will not hold, condition may have resulted from driving through a puddle. To dry out linings drive very slowly for a short distance with brakes lightly applied.

The same types of brake troubles are encountered with power brakes as with standard systems. Before checking the more expensive repairs in the power system, check out the usual braking problems.

Power brake test: Put your foot on the brake as you start the car. You should feel the pedal change to a softer action if the system is functioning properly.

Try your own adjustment. Most later model cars are equipped with a self-adjusting brake mechanism which works when the car is driven in reverse and the brakes are applied. If you don't drive in reverse very much, you may find excessive brake pedal travel. To fix, drive the car backward and forward a few times, applying the brakes after each movement. This should return the brake pedal to normal.

Finally, front linings always wear out before back brake linings—usually twice as fast. The repair shop usually will check only the front wheels and try to sell you linings for the brakes on all four wheels. Have the rear-wheel linings checked separately. You may not need to reline them. Brake linings can wear out after as little as 7000 miles if you drive with your foot riding the brake, but up to 70,000 miles if you treat them right. The master cylinder should last 30,000 to 50,000 miles, or more. Brake jobs commonly include rebuilding the wheel cylinders, but some mechanics say this is too frequent unless the brake fluid is seeping through to the cylinder.

Brake drums should last the life of your car. If your drums are faulty, however, it could cause you to go through linings rapidly. Sometimes drums get "out of round," that is, they get nicked or warped. This causes wear on the linings. The drums should be re-surfaced, and most shops have special lathes to do the job relatively inexpensively. One hazard here is that a mechanic might prefer simply to sell you new linings every several thousand miles rather than resurface the faulty drums.

Disc brakes generally need equivalent repairs, although the specific parts may differ from drum brakes.

What Your Tires Can Tell You

Tires should be inspected regularly for excessive wear, fabric breaks, or other damage. And while you are looking, you can do some troubleshooting.

Cupped tire: Caused by bad shock absorbers. The shocks do not have enough valve action and are allowing the tires to hop up and down on bumps. Look for patches gouged out all around the inside of the tire.

Feathered edge: Improper toe-in or toe-out of wheels. Corrected by wheel alignment.

Shoulder wear: If tires are worn on both sides, they need more pressure. Most good mechanics advise inflating tires a few pounds higher than the manufacturer recommends.

Middle wear: Over inflation. Best to check inflation when tires are cool since pressure can increase up to six pounds more when tires are hot from driving.

Irregular wear: If accompanied by a vibration of the tire when driving, which can be felt in the steering wheel, your wheels are probably out of balance. Mechanics will often try to sell new idler arms when you complain of a vibration in the steering wheel. Try a wheel balance first.

Excessive wear on one side: Improper camber, which means the wheels are tilted excessively inward or outward. Correct by alignment.

Patches on one side of tire: Wheels are out of balance.

If you have late-model tires, you can check for tread wear by looking at the indicators molded into the bottom of tread grooves in all new tires. When these smooth bands appear in two or more adjacent grooves, replace the tire.

With older tires, tread wear can be measured by using a penny to measure the depth of the tread. Insert Abraham Lincoln head first into the tread. If the top of Abe's head shows, the tread is worn and the tire should be replaced.

If you're in the market for new tires you should read the August 1971 issue of *Consumer Reports,* which has an exhaustive report on the different kinds of tires, their prices, what kind of tire is needed for various kinds of driving, and what safety factors you should consider. Tire guarantees are the emptiest around. By the time tread wear is pro-rated over the time you have used the tire, you end up paying for a new tire.

When getting a flat tire fixed, be sure you get a permanent repair. Many gas stations simply repair a puncture by externally inserting a rubber plug with a

Feathered Edge

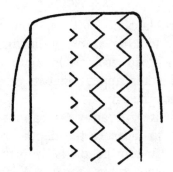

Excess Side Wear

Excess Center Wear

Abnormal tire wear

special gun-type device. This isn't a permanent repair and may not be safe. Insist that the tire be checked for possible internal damage and that any punctures be repaired with patches or rubber plugs inserted from inside the tire.

What to Watch Out For in the Cooling System

The cooling system consists of various hoses, plugs, caps, and clamps surrounding a radiator whose job is to keep your engine cool. Heat removed by the cooling system of an average automobile running at normal

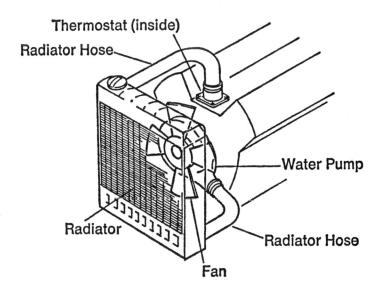

Cooling system

speed is sufficient to warm an entire house in zero weather.

The cooling system of today's car requires more servicing than that of cars of the past, thanks to the bigger and hotter engine propelling it. This gives the mechanic more chances to replace parts that don't need to be replaced. Knowing a few don'ts about the servicing of this system can save you money and an overheated engine.

Most cars should have a cooling check every fall to see if the system and coolant, now usually ethylene glycol (or permanent antifreeze) is ready to handle the dual job of guarding against overheating and preventing your engine block from freezing in winter weather. Ethylene glycol is mostly antifreeze, but it provides better year-round cooling for newer engines.

Rather than automatically draining and filling your cooling system with a new coolant each year, make this check. Run your finger around the radiator filler neck. If it is coated with brown sludge, the system needs flushing. Most extended-life coolants should last a couple of years and they often incorporate a color-changing chemical which tells when the coolant should be changed. Check the directions on the label to see what to look for.

Most gas stations will run a free check of your year-round coolant or, in older cars, antifreeze to see at how low a temperature it will protect your engine against freezing. You can check for yourself with a hydrometer or other inexpensive measuring devices similar to those described earlier for use in checking batteries.

Every two years, however, the radiator should be completely flushed and new coolant added. Otherwise, periodic checks of the hoses for bulges and cracks usually is all that is needed.

When it comes to cooling system maintenance, watch out for the following:

—Mechanics who point to a radiator hose with a little bit of play in it and say it is losing pressure. Actually, a radiator hose should feel like a beach inner tube filled to capacity, not like a rigid metal pipe. (This test only works on pre-1970 model cars.)

—A mechanic who wants to remove the radiator cap while the engine is hot. Once the cap is removed, the boiling point of the coolant is reduced and it will start boiling. Hot coolant will spill out, doing damage to other parts of the engine and to anyone nearby.

—Lazy mechanics will not drain out the old solution before adding the new. They simply drain out enough of the old coolant to make room for one can of the new. Then they charge you for the full amount your radiator can hold.

—Other mechanics will add water to your radiator. When your car has a coolant in it, water dilutes the solution and cuts down measurably on the effectiveness of the solution.

—Flushing the radiator is different from draining. It should be flushed every two years. If you want to make sure your radiator is flushed and not just drained, you can stick around the shop and watch to see that the mechanic drains out the old solution through the radiator drain valve. Then he should stick the valve back in and add enough water to fill the system. He should run the engine until a normal operating temperature is reached and then pull out the plug and drain the system again. He should do this until the drained liquid is colorless. Then he should add the ethylene glycol solution which will provide the required cooling and corrosion protection.

—When the system is only half flushed, the sludge and rust that have built up in the block will remain there and eventually restrict water passages. The engine will be difficult to start and the mechanic can sell you all kinds of repairs even though you only need to have the system flushed.

A clogged radiator is one reason your car may overheat, and draining the radiator should solve that problem. Here are other common problems and parts to check when your car heats up.

Radiator or hose leaks: If you see a whitish substance around the hoses, you probably have a coolant leak; a puddle under the radiator indicates a radiator leak. Rather than replace anything, pour a can of stop-leak into the radiator. The particles will mix with your coolant and, under heat and pressure generated by the cooling system, will fill the radiator cracks and weld them shut. If you are due for a coolant change, drain the old and install antileak ethylene glycol antifreeze.

Thermostat: This device is designed to close off the flow of water from the engine to the radiator until the engine has reached the desired operating temperature. It should last the life of the car, but sometimes it doesn't. If the thermostat gets stuck in an open or closed position it can cause your engine to boil over in the summer and keep your heater from putting out enough heat in the winter.

Water pump: This keeps the water circulating in a car's cooling system and may need to be replaced once before your car heads for the junkyard. It is one of the few items that is usually cheaper to replace than repair, though the cost still is more than just a few bucks. The "squirt trick" is not unknown to mechanics. When he points to a wet pump and says the hose is leaking, make sure that it really is. To check, start the engine, let it run for a while, and turn it off; then run your hand around the water pump. If it's wet, you probably need a new pump.

Radiator cap: This should be checked once a year or so to make sure it is maintaining the proper pressure. Otherwise, you'll lose the coolant or antifreeze from the radiator.

Fan belt: The fan belt also is part of the cooling system. But, in addition, it is an important part of your car's charging system and is discussed in the next section on—what else?—the charging system.

Air conditioners put a heavy load on a car's cooling system and, especially on older models, are a frequent cause of overheated engines. If you have one, keep a cool eye on it. But they are complex devices which have problems of their own and usually require professional attention.

A final warning on coolants. Car owners are being bombarded with advertising aimed at convincing them that the usual radiator solution isn't enough to do the job. The message: Keep your car running cooler with a radiator additive. Car owners have heeded the message to the tune of $10 million in sales per year for the coolant additives.

Andy Granatelli is the chief spokesman for the additive business. He, along with his wife, Dolly, spends a good bit of his advertising dollar pushing STP Keep Kool on radio and TV. Keep Kool is the number one seller among summer coolants.

What is disturbing about the newest Granatelli additive is that tests by Union Carbide, Dow Chemical, and the Federal Trade Commission indicate that these summer coolant additives are nothing more than a combination of antifreeze and water with some lubricant in it, a little soap and a bit of rust inhibitor thrown in for good measure—about the same ingredients as in a can of antifreeze (ethylene glycol). An authoritative magazine of the automotive trade, the *Automotive Cooling Journal,* broke with its usual industry line and called Keep Kool "largely the product of inspired advertising."

The Automotive Cooling Association's executive director, C. W. MacKenzie, was quoted in *Business Week* in its July 24, 1971, issue as saying that "None of these products will improve the cooling efficiency of an automobile's radiator nor will they protect the cooling system any better than the proper amount of antifreeze [ethylene glycol]." *Business Week* continued, "Moreover, antifreeze will do the job a lot cheaper, says MacKenzie. 'If you're puzzling over the cost of the material [in Keep Kool], about 20 cents will cover it, plus 15 cents for the can.' "

The suggested retail price for Keep Kool is $2.95 a quart. A good can of antifreeze costs about 80 cents less.

Adding their criticism to MacKenzie's are the auto makers who caution against adding anything extra to your car's cooling system.

It's doubtful that these summer additives could do much harm to your radiator since they contain little more than antifreeze. The one percent of extras allow the manufacturers to retire the dull antifreeze label for the alliterative eye-catching names—Keep Kool,

Kool-It, and Kwik Kool—and tack a dollar on to the price.

Similar doubts have been raised by auto companies and others about the usefulness of gasoline and oil additives. After testing Andy Granatelli's STP oil additive, Consumers Union reported in its *Consumer Reports* magazine that STP Oil Treatment, which basically thickens oil, is of little help to most older car engines and could void the warranty on some new cars by changing the viscosity of the oil "to a considerably thicker grade than certain auto manufacturers recommend." Granatelli, who responded by stepping up his advertising campaign, said the fact that people keep buying STP proves it does some good.

What to Watch Out For in the Electrical or Battery Charging System

The guts of your car's electrical system lie in the alternator (or, in some cars, the generator) and the voltage regulator. The battery acts as a storehouse for the electric current generated through the alternator/generator and the regulator.

Alternator: The alternator is a device that keeps the battery charged and has been used in American cars since 1963. It replaced the generator, which is still used in many foreign cars and, of course, in pre-1963 U.S. cars.

Voltage regulator: The voltage regulator controls the amount of electric current that flows through the alternator or generator. Frequently, the battery, alternator, or generator is replaced to no avail because an electrical problem is in the voltage regulator.

One sign of a faulty regulator is excess electrolite boiling out of the battery. The regulator is letting too much current get through the alternator or generator to the battery. If a bluish-green substance builds up on the battery within 150 miles after you scraped it off, the regulator probably is at fault and needs to be repaired, not the battery. The alternator or generator conceivably could be at fault, but problems with these devices generally are associated with undercharging, not overcharging.

If the battery water is drying up too quickly, or the battery is running down frequently, your car again may be getting too much of a charge from the voltage regulator. That's not all bad. A new voltage regulator is cheaper than a new battery.

Similarly, the voltage regulator may be suspect if grease or wetness appears on the battery top. First clean the top with a strong solution of detergent. If the stuff builds up again within 200 miles, don't buy a new battery, have the voltage regulator checked.

When a lack of adequate charging is traced to a bum alternator or generator, remember that such problems often involve only part of such devices. Buy a new or rebuilt one only after getting several opinions. Frequently, the problem is in the brushes, the brush spring, or the wire to the brushes, which is much cheaper to fix than buying a new alternator or generator.

In fact, before you authorize repairs for the regulator, alternator, or generator, have a mechanic check the regulator with a voltmeter while you watch. The mechanic should hold the car at a fast idle. Everything should be off (radio, wipers, and so on) except the ignition. If your car doesn't have heavy electrical equipment, such as an air conditioner, the voltage regulator should read 14.2 volts. If there is heavy equipment, 14.4 to 14.8 volts should be the reading. The voltage should not exceed this. If it does, you need a new regulator. If you get a battery instead, it will just run down again soon.

Fan belt. As mentioned in the previous section, the fan belt is also part of the cooling system. However, because it plays such an important part in the charging system, it is discussed here.

The fan belt drives the fan, the generator, and the water pump. It keeps the engine cool.

If the fan belt is too loose, it will slip, wear out fast, run down the battery, and overheat the engine. It is not good to have a loose fan belt.

It is not good to have a too-tight fan belt, either. This will cause rapid wear of the water pump and generator bearings.

It's a good idea to check your fan belt periodically for tension. To do this, see if the belt will move one half to three quarters of an inch toward the generator when you push the belt with your thumb. If it will, the tension is okay and you can count on the belt to do its job.

A worn fan belt is obvious—it's frayed around the edges.

Repairmen like to replace fan belts. There is a high markup on the part itself and most mechanics can beat the flat-rate time for the job.

Be sure to check your fan belt before leaving your

car at a garage. Many a motorist has been called in the middle of the day to be told that the fan belt needs to be replaced. Having no way of knowing, generally the motorist will say go ahead.

The other side of fan belt repairs is that when the problem actually is your fan belt, a relatively inexpensive repair, the mechanic can convince you the problem is the generator, alternator, voltage regulator, or battery—all more expensive repairs. You can look at your fan belt yourself and tell if it needs to be replaced or tightened when you have electrical system symptoms.

Remember: You should always start with the least expensive repair that could be causing your car problems and work up. The mechanic may start at the other end of the cost scale and work down.

What to Watch Out For in the Ignition System

Ignition problems are quickly noticeable because the car is hard to start or won't start at all. In such cases, you'll often be told the problem is a bum starter. The most unknowledgeable layman can see the logic in that, and then he gets socked with a $60 bill plus labor (and the labor charge is usually plenty) for a new starter when the problem is often a small part attached to the starter and called the solenoid.

The solenoid can usually be replaced for anywhere from $4 to $20. Your repairman can easily test the ignition system to see if the problem is, in fact, the solenoid rather than the starter by bypassing the solenoid and starting the car. He does that by placing a screwdriver across the two large bolts on the sole-noid. (*Caution:* the heavy current passing through the tool can cause severe burns.) This connects the battery directly to the starter. If the car starts that way but doesn't start without the direct connection, the problem most likely is in the solenoid.

The solenoid may only be rusty and dirty, or it may need to be replaced. In any case, it's a lot less expensive than a new starter.

There are other less-expensive-to-fix causes for starting problems. Among those parts to check are the following:

Wires: Check all the wires to see that they are not broken or loose. Tightening or replacing wires is

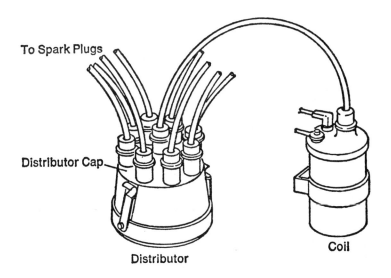

To Spark Plugs

Distributor Cap

Distributor

Coil

Ignition system parts

quick and inexpensive. But if you don't visually inspect first, a mechanic can tighten a loose distributor wire and charge you for a new distributor.

Distributor cap: This fits over your car's distributor. Loosen it and look to see if it's cracked. If it is, get a new cap for about $5. If it's just dirty inside, clean it out with a rag.

Distributor cap clips: If the cap is loose, it may be because one of the clips that holds it down has come off. The clip may have dropped down somewhere under the hood. If you can find it, put it back on. If not, improvise with a paper clip until you can get new clips.

Distributor points: Enclosed in the distributor, these open and close to make and break the ignition current some 150 million times in 10,000 miles of driving. They should be replaced every 10,000 to 15,000 miles. If you have trouble with points before 10,000 miles, have them adjusted instead. When the points aren't working right, your car will stall, miss, sputter, or not start at all.

Points may need to have the small peak that forms on one contact removed. This can be filed off; the points should then be dusted to make sure no loose particles remain. Discoloration, other than a slate gray, indicates burned points, which must be replaced.

As a precaution, the condenser, which smooths out the surges caused by the opening and closing of the points, is usually replaced when the points are.

Distributor and ignition coil should last the life of your car. Spark plugs, which we have already discussed, also are part of the ignition system.

What to Watch Out For in the Fuel System

Your car's engine is turning over, but it just won't start. Or else the car sputters or stalls or it hesitates when you press down on the accelerator pedal. You may not be out of gas according to your gas gauge, but you may be out of gas as far as your car's innards are concerned.

Before you rush out for a costly tune-up or major repair to cure your hard-starting or sluggish engine, there are several parts of your fuel system you should have checked first. Many are inexpensive to fix, and several you probably can even check for and repair yourself.

The carburetor: Though bad spark plugs and points can cause your car's engine to perform poorly, there also are several simple adjustments that can be made to the carburetor that may help—and save you a big tune-up bill.

There are two screws on either side of your car's carburetor which control how the car runs. The idle screw, located at the end of the linkage near the carburetor's base, and the air-fuel mixture screw, which is located on the other side. If the idle is too low to keep the engine running or too high, causing the engine to race, the idle screw should be turned out until the engine runs smoothly. The air-fuel mixture screw can be adjusted to give you the best mixture of gas and air while maintaining smooth idling.

Both parts should be adjusted at the same time and

after the car has had a chance to warm up. You can have the job done by a mechanic without getting socked with a big bill. No parts are involved and the labor time is minimal. There is less leeway for carburetor adjustments on newer cars with antipollution devices, but such adjustments can still be enough to make a difference.

The fuel lines: The problem could merely be that the fuel lines which carry gasoline to your engine are clogged. One easy check is to lift off the air cleaner and peer down into the carburetor while a friend tries to start the car. You should see little spurts of gas inside the carburetor if the fuel lines are clear. If you don't see any gas, you can make a further check by loosening the connecting tube between the carburetor and the fuel pump—the tube looks like a thin straw in most cars. Press the gas pedal or the lever next to the carburetor and see if gas spurts out. If it doesn't, that little strawlike pipe is crudded up inside.

After disconnecting the other end, blow into the straw and see if you can clear it out. Or stick a pipe cleaner in it and try to free the passage. Try pumping the gas again. If the gas comes out, put the tube back; gas should be getting to your carburetor.

If the gas line is clogged, the problem could be in the fuel filter, which is supposed to filter out dirt and sludge before it can get to the carburetor. (It also filters out water which may form from condensation when your car is out overnight with a near-empty gas tank.) On most cars, the fuel filter is a small, cylinder-shaped device which the fuel line between the fuel pump and carburetor runs through. The filter only costs a couple of bucks to replace and it should be replaced every year or two.

If the dirt, sludge, or water has gotten through your car's fuel lines and filter, the carburetor probably is dirty and needs cleaning. This happens only rarely, however, and carburetors hardly ever need to be replaced.

Other items to check for starting and sputtering problems include:

The air filter: This is supposed to prevent impurities in the air from getting to the carburetor when the air mixes with the gasoline to start and run your car's engine. After a while, it also can get clogged with dirt and keep the air from getting to the carburetor.

The air filter should be replaced every 10,000 to 15,000 miles, and a new one generally costs only about $2 to $5. You can even pick one up at a discount store or many drug stores and easily do it yourself. Just remove the lid of the air cleaner (that big pot that sits on top of the engine); the filter is that round thing with the honeycomb sides sitting inside. Take out the old one, put in the new one and screw the pot lid back on.

The PCV valve: PCV stands for Positive Crankcase Ventilation system, of which the valve is a part. But the letters are commonly described to mean Pollution Control Valve because the valve is part of a system used on American cars since 1963 to recycle some gas vapors back into the engine to be burned rather than spew out the tailpipe as pollutants.

If the valve sticks, or the ventilation system's hoses get clogged, you could have starting and stalling problems. A new PCV valve (along with a hose cleaning) costs only a few dollars and the valve should be replaced every year or so. A new valve frequently is included as part of a tune-up.

If you suspect the PCV valve is stuck, you can check it yourself. Take off the oil-filler cap (the filler is the place where you pour in oil) and put a piece of paper over the filler neck while the engine is running. The vacuum from the engine ought to hold the paper. If it doesn't the PCV valve is probably stuck.

The automatic choke: This device controls the amount of air that gets to the gasoline vapors in the carburetor. When the engine is warm, the butterfly plate on top of the carburetor should be open or the gas won't get enough air to start the engine. When the engine is cold, the plate should be closed or the air-gas mixture will get too much air and be too lean to start burning. But the plate always has to open a little to start the engine.

You can check to see if your automatic choke is working by taking off the air cleaner when the engine has warmed up. The butterfly plate on top of the carburetor should be wide open. If it is not, the automatic choke is either dirty or improperly adjusted.

You can get an aerosol cleaner to unclog the dirt. If the problem persists, you may have to get the choke cleaned or adjusted by a mechanic, but this is a minor repair.

The fuel pump: This is the device that pumps the gasoline forward from your car's gas tank to the engine. If it isn't doing its job properly, your car won't start or will cut out when you accelerate.

You don't want to fool with the fuel pump too much because that takes tools and some muscle. But one easy check is to take the cap off the top of the pump and clean out the crud that may have plugged up the screen under the cap. If that doesn't help, have the fuel pump checked by a mechanic. But don't have the pump replaced without checking the other, less expensive, fuel system problems mentioned earlier.

What to Watch Out For in the Exhaust System

The exhaust system consists of a pipe attached to a tin can containing sound-reducing baffles. The tin can is called a muffler.

Working inward, the exhaust system goes like this:

The tailpipe: Attaches to the muffler or connector pipe and is the part that you can see.

Connector pipe: Just an extension of the tailpipe—what you have if the tailpipe won't do the trick by itself.

Resonator: For big cars that need a heavy duty quieting. Actually a secondary muffler placed behind the main muffler.

Muffler: When you blow hard into a balloon, what you have coming back at you is called back pressure. Back pressure in the exhaust system strains the engine and causes fast muffler wear. Mufflers that perform best keep back pressure at a minimum through a series of baffle plates.

Extension pipe: Connects muffler with exhaust pipe to receive hot burned gas from the cylinders.

Exhaust manifold: Right next to the engine, it takes the hot air directly from the cylinders and transfers it to the pipes.

The whole system hangs together with bolts, washers, clamps, and hangers.

Mufflers have a relatively short life as car parts go, so many garages have jumped into the muffler repair business. There are several national franchised companies doing muffler repairs. These companies rely heavily on advertised specials and high-volume sales.

Of all the parts of the exhaust system, the exhaust manifold is the most expensive and the longest wearing. Mechanics will often try to replace it for you when repairing the exhaust system. The life expectancy of the rest of the exhaust system decreases as you work your way out—the muffler and the tailpipe are the fastest wearing.

When a muffler is shot, you can usually hear its rumbling noise. But don't let that be your only guide. Stifling noise is only part of the exhaust system's job. Another is to keep deadly—and silent—gases and fumes from getting inside your car. If you have any doubts, have the system checked before driving during the wintertime when most of the car windows usually are closed.

If you want to check the system yourself, some mechanics suggest the following: Start the car and let the engine idle; then stuff a rag into the tailpipe. If the car stops running, the exhaust system is tight. If the engine keeps running, you have an exhaust leak or leaks.

What to watch out for in muffler repairs:

—The kind of muffler to get. Several years back, ceramic-coated and stainless steel mufflers came on the scene but quickly vanished in a move by the muffler replacement franchises to get them off the market.

The reason: both mufflers are tough, stand up well to corrosion, and last a long time. The franchises make most of their profits from the incidence of muffler replacement such as clamps and hangers, plus a hefty service charge. Lighter coated mufflers with their more frequent rate of replacement fit this pattern of doing business so that today it is almost impossible to get a stainless steel muffler. About the best you can get is the zinc- or aluminum-coated muffler.

—If you can, stay away from cars with a dual exhaust system. Heat is what burns the corrosive acids off the parts of your exhaust system. With a dual exhaust, the parts never get hot enough to get rid of the corrosion. Besides, dual exhaust systems are twice as expensive as the regular kind.

—Clamps usually do not need to be replaced when the muffler does, but shops often do change them and charge you.

—Look carefully at the lifetime guarantee of those shops that base a lot of their advertising on mufflers that are "guaranteed for as long as you own your car." The muffler will be replaced but not the connecting parts—the clamps, hangers, and tailpipes— which can add a lot to your bill. Also, while they may install a muffler on your foreign car and hand you a guarantee, the guarantee expressly excepts foreign cars from "lifetime" coverage. Others charge an "installation" fee to replace the "guaranteed" muffler.

What to Watch Out For in the Suspension and Steering System

An ill-trained or dishonest mechanic can play on fear generated by a car that is not steering right to oversell ball joints, shock absorbers, and front-end components. Most mechanics will concede that ball joints are the most oversold item in the front end. A mechanic can get your car up on the rack and wobble your wheel to prove the joints are worn and loose

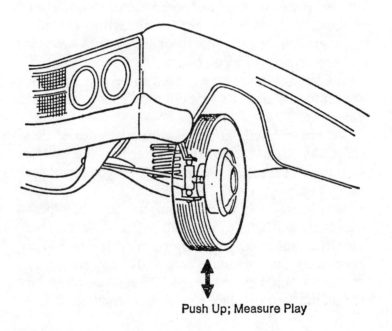

Push Up; Measure Play

Ball joint test

for a $50 repair bill. Actually, the joints will always be loose when the whole weight of the car is off them.

To test the ball joints, the car should be jacked up until just the wheel is off the ground. In that position, the only weight on the ball joint is the weight of the wheel, brake drum, and wheel assembly. The mechanic should lift the wheel straight up and down, so as to move the stud and ball up and down, and measure the movement. If it exceeds .050 inch the ball joints should be replaced.

Shock absorbers work with your car's springs to give you a smooth ride and stabilize the car. Under normal conditions, new shocks are needed at about 25,000 miles. If the shocks have seen 20,000 miles or so of driving or if a mechanic suggests new ones, give them the bounce test. Push down on one corner of the car. After bouncing back to its original position, the car should remain stable. If it continues to bounce up and down, the shock absorbers are not doing their job. Make the test on each corner.

On some newer cars, the bounce test won't work so well because of newly designed shocks. But another test you can try with any car is to find a deserted street, slow down to about ten miles an hour, and tap your brakes every few feet. If your car bounces up and down like a bucking bronco, you probably need new shocks. Another telltale sign is oil leaking from inside a shock (again, the leak should start from the top).

All four shock absorbers may not need to be replaced at the same time. But, for safety reasons, always replace the front ones and the rear ones in pairs.

Front-end alignment is often the repair suggested when a wheel balancing would do, for half the cost.

When your car begins to vibrate or thump down the road, you probably need a wheel balance. Also, look for cuplike depressions in the tire. Usually, only the front wheels need to be balanced. If your front tires wear more on one side than the other, your front end probably does need to be aligned.

What to Watch Out For in the Transmission

Modern automatic transmissions, capable of running 150,000 miles with good maintenance, are the most popular target of dishonest mechanics. But an alert driver can spot one a mile away. Keep in mind the philosophy of one of the biggest transmission gyp artists in the country:

—Transmission customers are a one-shot operation. Get them for everything the first time around.

—Anyone who comes to a transmission shop expects a big bill. Transmissions are a big item in the car. They'll never know that most things that go wrong are outside the transmission and can be fixed for a few dollars.

—Go all out on advertising. For some reason, car owners are particularly susceptible to specials on transmission repairs. Just get them into the shop.

—Always go out for a road test. You can make whatever is bothering the customer seem worse, and besides you can use this time to win his confidence.

—Never diagnose the problem before getting the car up on the rack. To get the customer into a bad bargaining position, have the car at least up on the rack with the oil pan off.

—When offering repairs, start with the $300 transmission overhaul with a lifetime guarantee. If that doesn't sell, offer the job with six-month guarantee for $200. If that doesn't work, offer the $150 special with the ninety-day guarantee.

Frankly, there is very little an individual can know about his transmission to protect himself from the fraudulent mechanic. A few troubleshooting techniques are listed here for what they are worth. The best thing to remember when going for transmission repairs is that as far as the transmission specialist is concerned you came down with yesterday's rain. He knows if he brings out his best salesman technique it won't be hard for him to sell you the works. The two most important things to remember when the transmission begins clunking:

—*Never* go to a transmission shop straight away. Go only when referred there by another mechanic who tells you what the problem is. Going to a transmission shop after hearing a noise is like heading for the heart specialist when you feel dizzy.

—Eighty percent of all transmission problems are minor and can be diagnosed and fixed without taking the unit apart.

Never, never let your transmission be dismantled without having a mechanic check the following parts on the outside:

1. Vacuum modulator
2. Oil filter
3. Pump intake circuit

4. Governor assembly
5. Detent solenoid
6. Control valves
7. Band adjustments
8. Linkage adjustment

Listening to your car is always a good idea, but it especially pays off where the transmission is concerned. The clunks, whines, and buzzes coming from the underside of the car are trying to tell you something. If you spot the problem early, it could save you hundreds of dollars.

Whine: Usually just means the fluid level is too low. Fill and watch the level. If you are losing fluid too fast (most cars use only a pint every 10,000 miles), you may have leaky seals. Check for reddish leaks. The seals can be repaired without taking the transmission apart. If you have been carrying heavy loads, the fluid may be worn out. Look at the transmission dipstick. If it has a deposit or if the fluid has changed color from its normal pink, replace the fluid and see if that doesn't correct the problem. You also may want to add a transmission sealant.

Clunking, or a loud kickdown as you come to a stop: Indicates loss of vacuum or a vacuum leak. You probably just need a minor adjustment to the vacuum modulator.

Loud slam: If, when you go from low to reverse, you get a loud slamming sound your problem is probably universal joints that need lubrication or are worn. They should be lubricated every 24,000 miles (about a $10 job). Some mechanics suggest you just leave them alone and replace them at about 75,000 miles for $35.

High-pitched buzz: Ninety percent of the time this is minor and indicates a stopped-up filter. To fix, change the filter and the fluid.

Two other frequently encountered transmission problems are minor:

Slipping gears: If you hear the engine momentarily racing as the gears change, a minor adjustment to the rings or band will probably take care of the problem.

Changing gears too early: Here the problem is not in the transmission at all. A simple two-minute adjustment to the throttle linkage on the carburetor to adjust the throttle pressure is what's needed. In this case the symptoms look serious but the cure is simple. A gas station attendant could make the adjustment for you. Inside a transmission shop, it would be an indoor sport to convince you your transmission needs an overhaul for $250.

Sometimes an automatic transmission will not change gears. This can be caused by the failure of a small gear on the transmission governor and can be fixed for $25 instead of a $200 "rebuilt."

Leaks: Transmission seals can break loose, but that doesn't mean you have to take the unit apart. Bad seals can be repaired without removing the entire unit. Look for a telltale red puddle under the car. Cost should be from $20 to $50.

A Detroit panel of service experts found that the most common cause of transmission malfunction is simply low fluid. On many cars, transmission fluid should be changed every 24,000 miles, more often if you carry heavy loads.

The good mechanic can make a lot of money servicing transmissions and many independents do just that. The franchised shops have a harder time of it.

The individual franchisee is usually a businessman who has found himself with $50,000 to invest. He invests it and then finds that after paying the high kick-in costs for advertising and promotion he's not making nearly as much as the brochure promised.

James F. Bere, president of Borg-Warner, one of the nation's leading transmission manufacturers, told Senator Hart's subcommittee that he changed his mind about setting up a Borg-Warner franchise of transmission shops because of the widespread abuses. He said he found that, although 90 percent of transmission repair is minor, most customers were being charged over $100 for transmission repairs no matter what the problem.

Mr. Bere said he learned about the overcharging in 1969, when he operated several repair shops in the Chicago area. Many customers were correctly being charged as little as $7 for adjustments to the transmission, he said. But other shops in the city would make the same adjustment, call it a transmission overhaul and charge $150. He concluded that under a franchise arrangement, he would not have the necessary control to keep such fraud from being perpetrated on unwary customers, and the franchising plan was dropped.

In one prominent case, the Federal Trade Commission charged AAMCO Automatic Transmission with falsely advertising cheap transmission repairs to attract potential customers who then "are frequently sold much higher priced jobs than reasonably necessary to restore their transmissions to sound operating condition."

Officials of a large transmission shop in Virginia give this advice: Never go to a transmission specialist unless you have been sent there by a mechanic you trust. And get more than one opinion on major jobs. You get estimates from painters and carpenters for their specialties, why not get estimates from mechanics when you may be spending a bundle for car repairs?

What to Watch Out For in the Engine

The engine is a fairly durable component of your car. That's good, because when something in the engine does have to be repaired, the job can be both complicated and expensive.

There is one engine repair that might be necessary if you own your car long enough. After about 70,000 miles, or maybe more, an engine may need a valve job costing in the area of $100. The symptoms: a sharp drop in power, a rough-running motor, and noise in the engine. These same symptoms could be caused by less expensive problems, such as dirty spark plugs. Have your mechanic make a compression check, and watch him do it. (In fact, a compression check should be done when you get tune-ups to spot valve trouble in advance.)

The purpose of the valves is to compress the fuel-air mixture in the cylinders to so many pounds per square inch (this varies from car to car) so that the spark plug can ignite it. By making a test of the compression rating for your car in each cylinder, the mechanic can tell if your valves are doing their job. If the rating between cylinders varies by more than 20 percent, you probably need a valve job.

You may have heard someone say in regard to his

engine that he "blew a rod." It doesn't happen all that often, but what the phrase means is that the rod that connects the pistons and crankshaft has crashed through the engine block. That's as bad as it sounds and usually calls for a new engine.

Blowing a rod usually stems from a loss, or lack, of oil to lubricate the many moving parts inside the engine. Fortunately, you can often tell when there is a defective rod because the rod will make a decided knocking or rattling noise when you accelerate from a stop or when you decelerate from a moderately high speed.

Major engine problems call for expert attention and can be too varied and complex to deal with in a book like this one. The best tack to take if told you need an engine overhaul or a rebuilt engine is to get a second opinion. You'll be spending several hundred dollars and you don't want to do that needlessly.

part three ———————————

Where to Go

chapter 8 _____

The New-Car Dealer

If your auto is still under warranty, all you have to do is head back to the dealer who sold you the car and all your repair worries will be solved, right?

Not likely. Consider the experience of a young secretary in Syosset, New York, with her 1970 Camaro purchased new in April of that year. By August, the car had been back to the dealer at least eleven times in a generally fruitless effort to get proper warranty repairs.

The secretary recounted her visits in a letter to General Motors, including such observations as:

—First, the "cute" gold Camaro "came with dents and scratches all over it" and was returned for a paint touch-up. The dealer painted the scratches, but "the color was too dark."

—Next, "the glove compartment wouldn't close. I brought it back two times for that and sometimes that doesn't work right."

—The car overheated "four times in four months" and was returned for a fourth repair attempt.

—The car was taken back "three times to get rid of a rattle in the dashboard" that is still there.

The secretary complained that when she returned the last time with her rattling dash, one repairman grumbled, "I pulled that car all apart to find that rattle and I'm sick of seeing this car come back."

Speaking for many frustrated new-car buyers, the secretary told GM, "Do you know how sick *I* am of bringing that car back?"

The auto makers, newspapers, government agencies, and consumer groups almost daily receive long letters from unhappy car buyers, listing page after page of complaints about warranty repairs, high charges for repairing other defects, and indifference on the part of the dealer and the manufacturer.

One Los Angeles man got so angry at the run-around he received from a Ford dealer and Ford Motor Company about fixing defects on his 1970 Lincoln Continental that he burned the $6500 car in protest on the Ford factory lawn there.

That's a bit expensive. But it dramatizes the complaints about warranty and other repairs performed by new-car dealers. A Federal Trade Commission study on auto warranties concluded that car manufacturers and dealers have failed to provide adequate repair services on both warranty and nonwarranty work. Those findings were more than confirmed at Senator Hart's auto repair hearings.

So before rushing back into the waiting arms of your dealer, consider the pros and cons.

There are pros. The biggest is that warranty repairs are free, if the dealer honors the guarantee. In addition, since he's likely to pay higher wages, dealers often have better access to the limited supply of skilled mechanics. Dealers also keep a large stock of parts and usually have the latest in specialized equipment.

Among the major cons is that for nonwarranty repairs, dealers, dollar for dollar, charge more than other kinds of garages. The markup for parts can go to as high as 70 percent, and the hourly rate for labor generally is higher owing to the dealers' higher overhead costs. And while warranty repairs are free, some dealers try to make up for the free fixes by finding nonwarranty repairs to make on your car, even if they aren't needed.

Obviously, not all dealers engage in the more dubious repair shenanigans; many try to give customers a fair shake on warranty repairs. But questionable tactics in both sales and service by dealers are widespread enough to have earned them a reputation as something less than angels.

Several years ago, pollster George Gallup made a nationwide survey to determine the public image for seven occupational groups: new-car dealers, bankers, druggists, supermarket managers, undertakers, service station managers, and plumbers. Gallup's interviewers asked respondents to: "rank these businessmen in terms of how honest and trustworthy you think they are." New-car dealers trailed every other occupation. Only 3 percent of those surveyed considered new-car dealers "most honest and trustworthy." Plumbers outscored dealers three to one, undertakers five to one, and druggists nearly twenty to one.

In a second survey, advertising executive David Ogilvy found that 54 percent of those polled thought the dealer had the best potential for service: he specialized in a certain make of car, had well-trained mechanics and a good stock of parts. However, a majority went elsewhere for service. Only 38 percent went to the dealer; they considered him untrustworthy, his prices high, and the waits too long.

The situation hadn't improved by 1970 when the

Federal Trade Commission, following up its warranty report, proposed that Congress pass a law to regulate federally the quality of both new cars and car repairs. However, Congress has failed to act on the FTC proposal, and the commission has undertaken a new investigation of warranties with an eye toward taking regulatory action on its own.

The 1972 Harris poll of consumer views showed that owners of U.S. cars still don't put much faith in car dealers. "American car owners favor their independent service station for ease, convenience and value of repair, while the imported car owners favor their dealer," Harris said.

To understand why such problems exist and how to deal with them, you need to understand how the system works. One fundamental flaw is that while car makers were pushing out millions and millions more cars onto the road, they expanded their service facilities in only a helter-skelter fashion. The four U.S. car companies distribute and service their cars today through just under 30,000 franchised dealers, who handle about 30 percent of all repairs. That's down from more than 40,000 dealers and 43 percent of the repair market in 1954, which explains why you have to wait so long to get in for service.

The Sales-Not-Service-Attitude

The reason for this state of affairs is that car companies are in the business to sell cars, not repair them. And the message—sell or else—comes through loud and clear to the dealers.

Technically, the dealer is an independent businessman. Rarely, however, does he have the capital to acquire more than a fraction of the value of property involved in the dealership. The rest is supplied by the manufacturer. Although the dealer may increase his ownership, rising costs of real estate, equipment, and facilities, plus expansion of the dealership, may keep him dependent on the manufacturer for a long time. Furthermore, he operates under a restrictive agreement with terms set by the manufacturer.

In the franchise agreement, often referred to as the selling agreement, a dealer contracts to sell and service the products of his manufacturer. The dealer does not receive an exclusive franchise for a given territory, but obtains a location for the sale and service of the product, which can be terminated at any time. The dealer promises to display and advertise the manufacturer's cars and trucks. He must also agree to stock parts, provide service to customers, and submit numerous reports on the business. He promises to meet a minimum sales quota set by the company. If he does not meet this quota, the franchise is subject to cancellation within thirty days.

An auto company's chief concern is sales—90 percent of its auto income is derived from new-car deliveries and only 10 percent from the sale of parts in connection with services. The auto makers often cancel a dealer's franchise for failing to meet sales quotas. But all reported to the FTC that they never have canned a dealer for failing to have adequate service facilities or for poor repair work.

Dealers are therefore pressured to be sales oriented and to adopt the auto makers' position that service is a necessary evil. The manufacturer normally selects as a dealer a person who is a salesman with some capital to invest and a good reputation in the community. The dealer soon learns that new-car sales is his bread and butter. He may receive bonuses for superior sales performance, but there are almost no financial rewards for good service.

The repair records of foreign-car dealers haven't been anything to gloat about, either. One possible exception is Volkswagen, which—unlike U.S. car makers —carefully increased its service facilities in line with its rising sales; but that doesn't mean some VW dealers aren't above taking advantage of an overly trusting beetle fan, and gripes about VW repairs seem to be increasing. Many other imported-car owners still suffer from hard-to-get parts and scattered dealerships, although the Japanese car makers, Toyota and Datsun, are rapidly expanding their facilities in the U.S.

One promising sign for the future is that Volkswagen has come up with a "Computerized Self-Analysis System" that plugs its cars into the computer age. Volkswagen, in effect, is building an electronic diagnostic system into its cars. Every VW built since mid-1971 has a special socket in the engine that is wired to sensors and probes inside the car. By plugging the car's engine into a computer, a mechanic can make more than sixty vehicle tests in about twenty-one minutes.

The plug-in unit potentially can reduce time-consuming inspections, human miscalculations, and, hopefully, repair costs. The computer check will be available at some VW dealers by fall 1972, and Volkswagen of America estimates that most of its 1200 U.S. dealers will be computerized by fall 1973. The program already has been tested successfully in Europe and very likely will be copied by U.S. car makers if it makes a good showing in this country.

Warranty Problems

The sales-not-service attitude is also behind the problems with extended new-car warranties. Such warranties were introduced in the 1960s basically as a selling tool. The car companies soon discovered, to their dismay, that customers actually expected the warranties to be backed up and that many ungrateful souls even complained about the numerous exceptions in the fine print. (Warranties typically don't cover such items as oil changes, tune-ups, front-end alignment, wheel balancing, or anything else which the dealer or manufacturer decides aren't "defects in material and workmanship in normal use.")

Since the companies found they couldn't live up to the warranties, coverage on most current cars has been cut back from a peak of five years or 50,000 miles to one year or 12,000 miles. American Motors, the smallest U.S. car maker, as much as conceded the insincerity of the industry's past warranty claims when it gambled that a warranty that really covered "everything" on its 1972 model cars would be a novel sales pitch.

A related reason for warranty troubles at the dealer level is that the car companies haven't properly reimbursed dealers for making such repairs. As a result, dealers don't like to do warranty work because they get only slightly more than a wholesale price from the manufacturer and considerably less than they would get from a paying customer.

If there is any disagreement between the manufacturer and dealer over whether or not the repair is covered by warranty, the customer is caught in the middle and left holding the bag—or a big repair bill.

What does all this mean to you? First, it means that since the dealer isn't likely to be too keen on doing warranty work, you often get shoddy warranty repairs on your car (and snooty treatment). A study made for the U.S. Department of Transportation by Operations Research, Inc., found that the comeback rate for warranty repairs performed by dealers is twice as high as nonwarranty repairs made by the same dealers. Repairs to "safety-critical" parts were adequate in only 77 percent of work done under new-car warranties, compared to 89 percent for the same repairs done in the same shops for customer-paid work, the study said.

Second, it means you pay more for nonwarranty repairs. Many dealers try to make up for what they lose in warranty repairs by overcharging the paying customer. Testifying before the Senate Subcommittee on Antitrust and Monopoly, T. A. Williams, president of the National Automobile Dealers Association, said:

We as dealers are not satisfied and do not feel that we are being properly compensated through the use of the warranty formula used by the various manufacturers. This is part of the reason why there is a difference in some dealerships between a warranty rate and a customer rate.

The Department of Transportation asked Booz Allen & Hamilton, Inc., one of the largest management consultant groups in the country, to analyze the hundreds of letters written to congressmen, senators, and government agencies complaining about shoddy auto repair. The letters typically carried copies of bills, work orders, and letters that had gone to auto industry officials listing the consumer groups and agencies to whom carbons had been sent—the consumers' chronicle of frustration and annoyance.

Of the 2206 complaints analyzed (most of which were made against automobiles purchased new from a dealer), 44 percent complained of excessive costs and unsatisfactory repairs. Booz Allen listed the reasons given for the dissatisfaction: misrepresentation of work performed (where the customer was charged for work which was not done, or for more hours than were actually used); use of the flat-rate manuals which encourage fast but slipshod repairs; profiteering manufacturers who set the price for parts at two to three times the cost; greed of dealers who set labor rates at $10 to $12 per hour even though the mechanic gets only $3 or $4.

As the Booz Allen and other studies show, some dealers go beyond mere price boosting to offset warranty repairs. They may perform phony repairs, charge for new parts when used parts are employed, put down more labor time than the repair actually takes, overcharge for parts, and engage in numerous other illicit repair practices. For such actions, the dealer is not held accountable by the auto manufacturer, who, in fact, condones, and in some cases encourages, such behavior.

The mechanic in this kind of dealership becomes part of the system. He can adapt himself to the unethical climate with few qualms, for he too feels that he is forced to work for small profits under the flat-rate system. One Texas car owner told the Senate investigating committee this story about a woman in

Dumas, Texas, who has a son who worked as a mechanic for a Pontiac dealer in Amarillo:

[He] had the job of looking over a fairly new Pontiac for a lady in Amarillo (who is fairly well to do) and with the understanding that she would leave it with them until repaired. The mechanic found some small item, worth eighty cents, faulty, and replaced it, marked the ticket "Labor, N.C." (no charge). The car was still there the following day, and the mechanic wondered why the lady had not come after her car; and the mechanic looked at the shop ticket, found that his eighty cent ticket had been replaced with parts and labor of various items, total of over sixty dollars. The shop foreman or owner was asked what the items on the ticket were for, and [the mechanic] was told that they couldn't make money on eighty cent items, and the lady in question "expected" to pay for service to her car, and this was the reason for keeping the car an extra day before calling her, and also for jacking up the repair bill. This mechanic called this woman and told her what the Pontiac dealer had done to her, and then quit his job.

This story is unusual only because the mechanic involved blew the whistle. Too many mechanics under these circumstances would keep their silence and their share of the booty.

Summary

Knowing their shortcomings, should you take your new car back to the dealer? The answer is yes, for some repairs. Many new-car owners say the free repairs you can get under warranty usually offset higher charges you might suffer for other repairs. Dealers are the only ones authorized to perform warranty repairs, and usually only the dealer who sold you the car will handle such repairs on your car. Ford requires you to have warranty repairs done by the selling dealer. It doesn't matter if his service is lousy.

You can protect yourself by not authorizing any nonwarranty repairs at a dealer until you shop elsewhere to see if the repair is needed and can be done more cheaply. Be especially careful when the dealer has your car in for a mileage checkup, a time when a mechanic is likely to look for nonwarranty repairs to make.

Remember especially that you can have routine maintenance required by the warranty—such as oil changes—done elsewhere, usually at lower costs. This won't invalidate your warranty, as some dealers imply.

There may be some times when you might prefer to seek nonwarranty repairs at the dealer, despite the higher prices. Dealers sometimes are better equipped to handle highly technical repairs in the electrical system, in power accessories, and other specialty areas. They usually have the latest equipment and instruction bulletins from the factory, and the mechanics usually have more experience on the brand of car sold by the dealer.

One other possible exception is if, by luck, you happen on a dealer who really is interested in performing good service. In almost every town there are dealers who, aware of the industry's rotten repair reputation, emphasize service as a unique selling point. The prospect of reliable, skilled service might be important enough to you to offset the likely higher costs. But such dealers are hard to find, and especially can't be turned up through dealer advertisements. Check with neighbors and friends.

If it's not too late for you, one way to guard against postsale warranty and repair woes is to check out the dealer *before* buying a new car. Ask to look at his service facilities and check around to find out what kind of reputation he has for service. In many cases, some auto company officials say, the high-volume dealer who relies heavily on showroom traffic for sales pays less attention to service than the lower key dealer who depends on repeat customers and referrals.

One way you can check a dealer's service attitude before buying that new car is to call the service shop and pretend that you want to bring a newly purchased auto in for warranty repairs. If they ask you to make an appointment far in advance, or otherwise put you off, take your buying business elsewhere.

One last precaution is to think about how repairable a car might be before you buy it. According to Ralph Nader, a large proportion of auto repair costs would not be "as expensive or even necessary if key parts were not so inaccessible or fragile, or so constructed that a small defect requires replacement of an entire large unit of the car."

You have no way of telling what little parts inside the engine fall into this category. But you can avoid some of the more obvious, and generally unneeded, features that are likely to be expensive to fix, things like retractable headlights, power brakes, oversized engines, speed-control units, and power windows. A reliable source for new-car buying is the annual *Auto Buying Guide* published by Consumers Union in its *Consumer Reports* magazine.

chapter 9 ─────────────

The Independent Garages

If you look hard enough, you may find a top mechanic doing repair work at reasonable prices in your own neighborhood. Chances are, he doesn't advertise, his garage is small and crowded, and he depends on repeat business and the recommendations of satisfied customers. He is an independent garage owner.

There are two basic types of independent garages. One type encompasses the large independents, many of which specialize in foreign cars or a particular U.S. make. These shops mass-produce service and often are close behind dealers in obstinacy and poor quality control. Such independents, however, generally charge less than dealers although they have almost as much access to parts and mechanics.

The more common type of independent shop owner, however, is the fellow with that small, crowded garage. The typical independent garage does less than $40,000 worth of business a year. The owner often is a mechanic who works at the garage full time. He may employ one or two others, and he generally trains them himself. He is more likely to worry about his customers because they are his only advertisement, and he needs their repeat business.

Because the small garage owner has lower overhead costs and generally charges a lower labor rate than a dealer, his prices are lower than dealers'. On the other hand, he can't do the volume business of a specialty shop or big independent, nor can he wangle big discounts on parts purchases as mass merchandisers do, so his prices might be somewhat more for certain repairs performed by those outlets.

Overall, however, small-garage prices usually are competitive. Although such garages can't get volume discounts when buying parts, they generally purchase parts made by independent parts makers, or rebuilt parts, rather than the more expensive ones made by the auto companies. And the independent parts are just as good. Moreover, the garage owner often provides the extra value of personalized service and is more receptive to resolving complaints when they do arise.

Such garage owners, however, may be a disappearing breed. There are approximately 112,000 independent repair shops across the country. Just ten years ago, there were nearly 140,000. Many independent garage owners have been squeezed out by large auto dealerships, giant department stores, and franchisers who attract the high-volume and quick-turnover repairs, leaving the independents with the hard or unprofitable jobs.

The Parts Problem

Car dealers, in fact, do a lot to see that independent garages have a hard time getting some parts. With help from the manufacturer, dealers control certain auto parts in their areas. Independent garage owners must go to the local franchised dealers of different car models to secure body parts and certain single-source items, such as transmissions.

In the mid-1960s the Federal Trade Commission filed suit against the major auto manufacturers on the grounds that their practice of selling parts only through their dealers was forcing 25,000 independent repair shops into an uncompetitive position. As matters stood, the independents, forced to buy parts from the dealers in the area who were competing with them, found the parts largely unavailable. And when the dealers did sell the parts, they tacked on an exorbitant charge for playing middleman. When the auto manufacturers agreed to start paying their dealers for distributing the parts to the independents, thus making them available, at least in theory, the FTC dropped the suit.

Now, almost ten years later, testimony before Senator Hart's subcommittee indicates that the dealers are not living up to their side of the bargain. Independent garage owners testified that "captive parts" are as hard to get as ever. The FTC is back in the picture looking at unfair restraints of trade and rebates in the auto industry with an eye toward solving the problem once and for all by forcing the manufacturer to sell these parts directly to the independents.

Will Your Warranty Be Invalidated?

The auto manufacturers and dealers also have thrown up smoke screens regarding the new-car warranties that hamper the independents and other non-dealer repair outlets. The purpose is to convince owners to return their cars to the dealer for all maintenance work rather than take them to a garage that will do the work for less. Knowing what service doesn't have to be performed by the dealer under the warranties can save you money on maintaining a new car.

Largely through advertising, the car companies and their dealers have successfully conveyed the impression that only franchised dealers can perform the routine maintenance work required under the warranty. The fact is that such maintenance can be done by any garage without invalidating the warranty. Such maintenance includes oil changes, servicing the crankcase ventilating system, brake servicing, tune-ups, transmission linkage and band adjustments, and similar routine repairs.

Another problem generated by the auto industry is the widely held belief that only genuine "factory" parts can be used to replace worn parts or else the warranty will be invalidated. The fallacy in that old car-dealer's tale is pointed out in a story told by Robert Straub, past president of the Independent Garage Owners of America, and owner of the Modern Auto Service Company in Cleveland.

Mr. Straub's garage agreed to replace an engine in a Ford Mercury Comet for a customer. Mr. Straub got the replacement engine from his local Mercury dealer. He installed the engine and, of course, put in a new oil filter. When the engine was started, there were noises that indicated internal problems. Mr. Straub took the car over to the Mercury dealer who sold him the engine and had the assistant manager take a look. The first thing the assistant manager said was that although the engine appeared faulty, the warranty on it would not apply because Mr. Straub hadn't installed a Ford oil filter, but had put in a Fram filter.

The story didn't end there because Mr. Straub, as a garage owner, knew about the auto parts industry. For a regular customer who had installed a non-Ford filter on his car the book would have closed. But Mr. Straub knew that Fram had a contract to manufacture oil filters for Ford Motor Company. The only difference between the Ford filter and the one Mr. Straub had put in the car was the label.

The moral is that even if a replacement part isn't an original-equipment "factory" part, it may be as good as original equipment which keeps the warranty in effect. A "factory" part means only that it was made by, or for, an auto company, and it probably costs more. Independent parts manufacturers, and there are hundreds of them, make replacement parts which equal and, in many instances, surpass the quality of so-called genuine parts.

For example, if you go for routine maintenance to a garage and get Champion spark plugs installed on your car, the warranty isn't invalidated. Champion spark plugs are as good as Autolite (Ford's spark plugs) or Delco (General Motors') or those of any other car maker. The same applies for other equipment. (In early 1972, the Supreme Court upheld a government antitrust suit ordering Ford to sell off its spark plug business.)

Naturally, only car dealers can do warranty repairs. But, if you'll check your warranty book closely, you'll see what maintenance, required to keep the warranty in effect, can be done elsewhere. Normally, you will have to provide proof, in the form of receipts, that the work was performed. These usually must be presented to the dealer at required intervals. This has the

practical effect of assuring the manufacturer that you
are living up to your part of the warranty terms. It
also is an effective tool for discouraging you from
taking maintenance work elsewhere; you may not
want to put up with the nuisance of keeping receipts.
However, if you'll check your warranty book, this no
longer may be such a nuisance. Although it isn't
widely advertised, the warranty books of most car
makers now contain coupons which can be filled in by
the garage performing the various mileage checkups
to certify that the work has been done. All you have
to do is turn them over to the dealer.

Advantages

The various maintenance services under the warranty can be performed at almost any type of garage.
But the one place that's most likely to be equipped to
handle the most all-around repairs on both new and
older cars at reasonable prices is the independent garage. The reason is a simple one. Car dealers make
money mainly by selling cars, gas stations pump gas,
and specialty shops concentrate on one or two repairs.
Independent garage owners have nothing to sell but
fixing cars, period; otherwise, they are out of business.

Nevertheless, independent garages, too, must be
chosen carefully. Some of them, especially larger ones
that don't depend heavily on repeat business, can oversell repairs to trusting motorists. Small independents
sometimes have trouble getting parts quickly—causing
long delays in getting your car back. And the fact that
a mechanic owns his own garage doesn't necessarily
mean he's a highly trained repairman.

The advantage for the consumer is that a bad, small independent doesn't last long because he depends mainly on word of mouth for advertising. Find one with a good reputation and you'll likely find dependable service at reasonable prices, although perhaps not the cheapest around. The personalized service offered by such a shop, however, may save you the difference between a big bill for an unneeded repair at a high-volume shop where you never see the mechanic and a minor repair at the local garage where everybody knows your name.

The independents also have organized to expand their services by forming the Independent Garage Owners of America. Among other things, the IGOA has adopted a nationwide warranty plan for independents which can benefit traveling motorists. Although most independents stand behind their work, there previously wasn't any way for customers to get their car repaired away from home when it broke down after being fixed at a local independent shop.

Under the new program, when a driver has his car repaired at an IGOA member garage, he can get a warranty certificate along with his receipt. If the same problem shows up when he is out of town, the motorist may have the car repaired at any IGOA member garage without cost to him. The shop that made the initial repair then is billed for the charge. Besides aiding travelers, such a system also puts pressure on IGOA members to maintain high performance standards.

chapter 10 _____

The Specialty Shops

Franchisers and specialty shops are just about synonymous in auto repairs today. A few years back, several businessmen foresaw the possibilities of high-volume, quick-turnover services for transmissions, brakes, mufflers, and other common repairs. They jumped into the auto repair business by franchising shops specializing in one type of repair and operated by individual investors under the franchiser's name. Examples of some better known, coast-to-coast franchised specialty chains today include Midas Muffler, and AAMCO Automatic Transmissions.

Today franchised specialty shops number more than 50,000, and their numbers are growing by about 6 percent a year, mainly at the expense of independent garages.

One lure of the specialty shop is the promise of quick service at lower prices. But much of the attraction the franchisers hold for the motoring public is directly due to their high volume of advertising. A substantial percentage of this advertising can be classed as misleading or bait advertising. Consider this ad:

Well, that's me, old Leo Durocher. I'm a baseball man and I look after the Cubs. Well, this fella here, he's a transmission expert. My friend from AAMCO. He looks after your car's transmission. Most cars over two years old need some transmission service. I say take your car to AAMCO, where many transmission problems can be fixed with a simple adjustment of bands or linkage. At AAMCO, $4.50. If your trouble is serious, you may need AAMCO's safeguard service. That's only $13.75. Includes AAMCO's multicheck, new transmission fluid and all minor adjustments. Just $13.75 fixes any sick transmission. Fixes yours or your money back on the spot. So see the experts. AAMCO, over 200 shops from coast to coast stand behind every AAMCO job. There's free towing and one-day service. So you see the nearby AAMCO this week and tell them Leo sent you.

AAMCO has not been the only advertiser of fantastic bargains. Midas Muffler has the touch, too, in advertisements such as the following:

You can keep your car forever and never have to buy another muffler. That's what the Midas guarantee means. Guarantee . . . no charge for installation, it's free! Nothing evasive. No fine print doubletalk. It says "guaranteed for the life of your car."

These are not the ads of fly-by-night operators. AAMCO and Midas are multimillion-dollar corporations, doing business in almost every state. Both AAMCO and Midas have been accused by the Federal Trade Commission of engaging in false and misleading advertisements and deceptive statements, all to the prejudice and injury of the public. The FTC's complaint against AAMCO went beyond false advertising to what the commission charged were deceptive acts and practices that AAMCO established as its "plan or method of doing business," which the franchisees were obligated to follow in order to keep their franchise. According to the FTC complaint, the method worked like this:

—When a customer telephoned AAMCO, he was informed that it was impossible to diagnose the transmission trouble by phone. He was further informed that the trouble may be minor and require a simple adjustment. He was offered a free test or checkup.

—Upon arriving at the AAMCO transmission shop, the automobile was road tested and checked. The customer was then advised that the problem was inside the transmission and consequently it would be necessary to remove, dismantle, and inspect the transmission. No bona fide effort was made during the road test or checkup to diagnose the problem. "The sole object of this procedure is to persuade and induce the customer to transfer custody of his automobile to the AAMCO shop so that he may be subjected to efforts to sell him an 'AAMCO custom rebuilt' transmission or other products or services at prices greatly in excess of the low prices offered in the advertisements," the FTC complaint said.

After a customer transferred his car to AAMCO, the FTC added, the transmission was taken apart and the sell begun, starting with the AAMCO custom rebuilt with a lifetime guarantee for $350. Should the customer resist, AAMCO offered the six-month guarantee, then the ninety-day guarantee until the sale was made. If the customer refused repairs altogether, AAMCO would refuse to reassemble and replace the transmission in its former condition.

The FTC complaint concluded that the AAMCO plan or method of doing business deprived customers of the opportunity to choose freely the services they needed. They were frequently sold much higher priced repairs than necessary to restore their transmission to sound operating condition. The plan was devised to place the customer in a disadvantageous bargaining position through fraudulent misrepresentations.

The FTC issued a similar complaint against Midas and its franchisees, citing it for misleading advertising. The FTC accepted consent orders to settle each case, prohibiting AAMCO and Midas from using deceptive sales schemes or devices and making false and misleading statements.

A consent order is sometimes considered little more than a slap on the wrist. In effect, the charged corporations say: "I didn't do it, but I won't do it again," and the complaint is settled. Of course, the FTC is supposed to enforce these consent agreements, but FTC employees say they need three times as many people as they have in the compliance office to make such agreements effective. Much of the compliance is left up to the corporation itself and it is only when, by some stroke of fortune, noncompliance is brought to the attention of the FTC that it investigates.

Letters to the President's Office of Consumer Affairs and personal investigation in the Washington, D.C., area indicate that the very reasons for which the complaints against AAMCO and Midas were issued continue. Midas still bases much of its advertising on its slogan "guaranteed for as long as you own your car," which is not a complete guarantee since a Midas customer who returns for a new muffler is charged for "service." Recently, however, Midas has been mentioning this installation charge in its advertising.

On June 8, 1970, the FTC barred AAMCO from

using allegedly deceptive practices and issued eighteen points for compliance. In the first year after the order, complaints against AAMCO were so heavy that the FTC attorney on the case considered taking AAMCO to federal district court to force compliance. Although complaints have continued to come in (as of November 1972), the new attorney handling the case finds that his understaffed compliance division cannot track down sufficient evidence to prove that AAMCO is in noncompliance with the 1970 order.

Tips on Using the Specialty Shops

Despite the frequent high-pressure sales tactics, specialty shops can be useful for the knowledgeable motorist—if he sticks to the repair he came in for. The high-volume, quick-turnover (and impersonal) service means such shops often can offer lower prices for their specialties than do other repair shops. And the service usually is pretty fast.

As mentioned in the section on transmission repairs, there is no sense in going to a specialist unless you are referred there. If you go to a brake shop because your brakes are pulling to one side, the mechanic probably will fix your brakes since that is what he is there to do. You may never find out that your car was pulling because of uneven pressure in your tires. The same goes for other specialty shops—they are only good for one kind of repair. The minute you drive in the door, your car has likely been diagnosed as having the problem they have the cure for, be it brakes, alignment, transmission, or carburetor.

If you do plan to visit a specialty shop for a needed repair, wait—if you can—until the repair you want (brake relining, alignment, tune-up, etc.) is advertised at a "price savings." You probably won't have to wait long because such "price savings" are advertised so frequently that they are just about the usual price for such repairs. Again, just be sure you don't let yourself be sold repairs beyond the advertised special without making sure you need them.

One last caveat for those who venture to see a specialist. Look twice at his guarantee; often the fine print reveals you've got more of a liability and less of a good deal. Most guarantees require that you return to that shop for periodic service to keep your guarantee in effect—thus giving them added opportunities to sell you repairs. And usually there is a service charge, which closely resembles what a labor charge would ordinarily be. By the time they calculate the use you have gotten from the part they had installed, you end up paying most of the price again.

Accessory Shops

Some light repairs—alignments, tune-ups, brake jobs, etc.—are offered by stores that retail auto accessories, replacement parts, and tires. There are more than 20,000 of them and many are franchised by tire manufacturers like Firestone, Goodyear, General Tire, and B. F. Goodrich.

The same caveats that apply to specialty shops generally apply to accessory stores. Often these outlets advertise bargains such as a free wheel balance and alignment if you buy a new set of tires. These specials can be good, provided you can resist the hard sell to buy a different set of tires—the ones not on sale.

The basic rule to remember is that accessory and tire stores are primarily in business to sell accessories and tires, not repairs.

(If you do need new tires, however, an outlet specializing in tires can be a good place to go. Such stores can usually buy tires from the manufacturer even more cheaply than mass merchandisers, so their prices generally are about the lowest around. Tires are heavily discounted items and "sales" are frequent, especially just before holidays such as Memorial Day and Labor Day.)

The Mass Merchandisers

Anyone who has been to a large suburban shopping center knows that the big department stores have gotten into the automobile repair industry with a vengeance. From a small outlet in Chicago in 1931, Sears Roebuck garages have grown to 5 percent of the big retailers' total business. It now has over 800 service outlets. There are at least a dozen other large merchandisers—S. S. Kresge's K-Mart, J. C. Penney, Montgomery Ward, E. J. Korvette, to name a few—who have unleashed their buying power and marketing expertise on the car owning public.

The auto repair market traditionally has been left to the small businessman in the corner garage or the new-car dealer. Rather than be put off by tradition, the department stores pinpointed the weaknesses in the present system—insufficient new-car dealer service shops, disorganized independent garage owners with poor bargaining power in buying parts and antiquated business practices, oil companies whose main interest is pushing gas, and the inconvenience of the established garages.

While the independent garagemen are often first-rate mechanics, they make poor merchandisers and businessmen. With the department stores, it is the other way around. Superb at merchandising, able to

119

buy parts below cost, and already established, the department stores quickly claimed ground in the once exclusive territory of the new-car dealer and small businessman mechanic. They concentrate on the high-turnover items such as batteries, tires, spark plugs, and mufflers; accessories such as floor mats and mirrors; and quick-service repairs such as brake service and wheel balance.

With their high-volume buying muscle, the mass merchandisers can get a better buy on such parts than anybody. They are the only repair operations that buy directly both from the auto makers and independent manufacturers. Since their sales also are high volume, such retailers can afford to sell the auto parts and accessories at lower markups, which means lower prices to you. Auto repairs now account for an average 5 percent of the volume of stores with repair outlets.

Convenience plus easy credit plays an important part. Indeed, a major advantage of the mass merchandisers is their location in the shopping center. An individual who goes to a repair outlet in a shopping center can leave the car, go do his shopping, then return to his waiting automobile and charge the whole business—all in all a less painful way to get the car fixed than a wait in a noisy shop. Despite their love of cars, Americans have always preferred department stores to garages.

There are drawbacks to all this speed and efficiency. Mechanics at the large department store outlets are usually thinly veiled salesmen or inexperienced beginners who each learn to perform one operation—one learns to install batteries, another to balance wheels, etc. They generally are not prepared to diagnose troubles. This quick-stop service is for the customer who knows what he wants. Many car owners will find out at their corner gas station that they need a battery, then go off to Sears and buy one, usually below the cost of buying one at the gas station.

Trained salesmen-mechanics at department stores are experts at pushing parts. Take the experience of a Washington, D.C., doctor who took his 1970 Cougar to Sears for a front-end alignment and then went shopping. When he returned, he was presented with a bill for $125 covering the cost of front-end alignment, replacement of ball joints, replacement of the idler arm, and new shock absorbers. The good doctor was shocked since just that morning he had taken his car to a District of Columbia inspection station for its annual safety inspection. Specifically, the shock absorbers, ball joints, and idler arm passed. The only failure was the front-end alignment which was his reason for going to Sears.

The Sears salesman had not yet replaced the shock absorbers when the doctor returned, and he could not show where the shocks were defective. The doctor paid his bill for $81.45 (less the cost of new shocks) to get his car back. Then he asked Sears to credit his account $72.57 ($81.45 less $8.88 for alignment) since the additional repairs were not authorized and according to state inspectors were not needed. Sears did not agree, and the doctor was left with little recourse but small claims court.

Some lawyers feel you have a better chance of getting your money back from a repair outlet operated by a large department store than from a small garage or dealer. If the repair is charged and you are a good customer, the store may not want to lose your business over a disputed auto repair bill, especially when they may be in the wrong. Large department stores generally have a reputation to protect and are more likely than a mechanic to adopt at least a the-customer-is-sometimes-right stance. But you still may have to make some noise and complain to get your due.

On the other hand, if you do not pay the part of the bill you feel is unjust, the store may take the other tack and injure your credit rating by canceling your charge account. And, if you take the dispute to court, you may find yourself face-to-face with a high-priced corporation attorney, not the mechanic or salesman who caused the problem. Unless you, too, hire an attorney, you may find yourself at a great disadvantage.

Also, don't get too excited about the widely advertised "guarantees" of the big retail chains on auto accessories. On closer reading, they often lose their appeal.

Consider, for example, Sears Roebuck's "tread wear-out guarantee" on new tires. In practice, it guarantees very little. Say you buy a new tire for $25 that is guaranteed to wear for twenty-four months. Twelve months later, the tread is worn down and you go back to collect on the guarantee. Under Sears's policy, all you get is a 10 percent allowance on "the current selling price" of the same tire. If it's still $25, you get all of $2.50 off the price and the privilege of paying another $22.50 plus tax for a new tire to replace your year-old one that was "guaranteed" to last two years.

If you bought your worn-out tire on sale, you're in

even worse shape. The discount still is off the "current selling price." So if you paid a sale price of, say, $20 for that tire which now sells at $25, the 10 percent discount means you'll pay $22.50 for the replacement tire. In other words, not only don't you get any discount, but you have to pay $2.50 more for the replacement tire than the original "guaranteed" one cost you.

In summary, the large department stores have excellent access to parts and probably the best prices for them in town. If you know what you need, you can probably save money purchasing it there. Independent tests have shown that Montgomery Ward and Sears batteries are good for the money; if you put in your own spark plugs, oil, fan belts, and shocks, get them there too. But if you have real mechanical trouble and you need some analysis of what's wrong, go to a mechanic, not a salesman; you'll be better off.

Gas Stations

Gas stations used to be just "a nice place to visit" for gasoline and maybe an oil change. Now, more often than not, service stations perform most major repairs.

Service station owners have found that repairing cars is more lucrative than just pumping gas. Also, gas station attendants have a lot of spare time between fill-ups. What better way to use it than repairing the cars of their ready-made customers.

The attraction for consumers is that the corner gas station is often more convenient and accessible than other garages. There are more than 200,000 service stations in the U.S. and they account for about 15 percent of the auto repair business.

The problem, however, is distinguishing which among those 200,000 stations are merely trying to keep attendants busy and make some extra money on repairs, and which are serious about the repair end and employ a knowledgeable mechanic.

The trend today is for mechanics to leave large dealerships and garages to head for small gas stations where they have more independence. They also can make better money if the repair business is substantial. Some of these mechanics even acquire service station franchises themselves and operate as owners.

When this is the case, having repairs performed at a gas station offers greater convenience, economy and, generally, more individual attention. It usually is easier to go back and talk to one mechanic at a gas station than it is to work your way down from the service manager to the mechanic, or up to the president, trying to get your car fixed properly at a new-car dealership.

At many stations, however, repairs are handled only by the attendant or a would-be mechanic. Unfortunately, many drivers tend to credit gas station attendants with more knowledge than they deserve when it comes to car repairs. Most gas station mechanics are self-taught, using the trial and error method on ailing cars of gas customers. Many times the service station attendant on duty the longest assumes the post of mechanic, or the conscientious gas-pump jockey moves from the pump to the service bay. When this happens, the service station loses a good attendant and gains a bad mechanic.

Cars are complicated. Although hanging around gas stations may be enough training to get the attendant through oil changes, battery replacements, and tire patches, it doesn't qualify him to dismantle your car's engine or overhaul the transmission.

The quality of service offered by the local gas station may also depend on the control exercised by the parent oil company when it leases the station to an individual operator. Some franchised operators are tightly controlled and pressured to mainly pump gas or lose their businesses. Other independent contractors have more freedom and can spend more time on repairs.

Generally, the gas station that is located at the

intersection of two major thoroughfares is not likely to give you the most for your money in repairs. He is probably in competition with three other gas stations at the same intersection and may have been given his franchise for the express purpose of pumping gas and pushing repairs on the traveling public. As mentioned earlier, gas stations that rely on travelers for business are more apt to engage in shady practices. Stations that can push tires or batteries on unsuspecting motorists don't want to take the time to perform complicated repairs.

There is one advantage of the service station franchise system: if you can't get satisfaction from the service station, you can look to the parent corporation. Many unhappy car owners have been successful using this tactic.

In most other ways, gas stations are similar to independent garages. They pay more for parts than dealers do but they have fairly good access to parts (though they usually keep only a limited supply on hand). Most mechanics at gas stations are paid by the flat-rate manual. Few are salaried. Attendants generally are paid by the hour. The labor charge at gas stations is below the labor charge at dealers. But you pay more for accessories like tires and batteries.

The quality of the equipment used by gas stations varies widely. Some have only enough to get by with relatively minor repairs like tune-ups, relining brakes, and wheel balancing. Others have invested in the gear and tools needed to perform heavier repairs in the engine and transmission.

Specific conclusions about the repair offerings of more than 200,000 gas stations are impossible to make. Although all pump about the same quality of gasoline—despite extravagant brand claims about performance differences—they serve up a widely mixed quality of repair services.

The decision on whether or not to trust your car to a gas station for repairs must be an individual judgment based on your evaluation of a particular station. Generally, the advantages are that repairs at gas stations are convenient and relatively inexpensive. If you become known as a regular customer, you're likely to get fair treatment and personalized service. While some gas stations on major highways have great opportunities to engage in shady practices, neighborhood stations are part of a community and tend to rely on repeat customers for most of their business.

You can find out whether your local station has a qualified mechanic—rather than attendants only—handling repairs and what kind of equipment it has. Even if it is equipped to handle only minor repairs, the mechanic may be willing to advise a regular customer when a major repair really is needed that must be made elsewhere and then let him know later if the repair really was made.

Where to Go—A Summary

There is no *one* best type of garage to take your car to for repairs. This book can only deal in generalities based on the records of performance by the various types of outlets. The research indicates that, on an overall basis, the small independent shop is probably the best all-around bet for most repairs.

But where you should take your car depends on

individual circumstances—such as the type of repair needed, the business methods of the specific outlets in your area, and your experiences with individual garages, gas stations, and dealers.

The overriding factor in your decision is likely to be the mechanic himself. One reason for auto repair problems is that there are too few skilled people to properly fix the ever-growing number of cars. Currently, there is an estimated shortage of 70,000 mechanics in this country, and the situation isn't improving. One reason for the shortage is low pay, although a good mechanic increasingly can earn a good living. But the main reason, ironically, is the low social status of an auto repairman in a nation that worships automobiles.

Despite the abundance of auto repair chicanery, there are thousands of hardworking and honest mechanics. Perhaps the best advice is to search one out wherever he may be and hang on to him for your repair business. When you take your car into the fix-it shop, insist on having it cared for by that mechanic, just as some people rely on a favorite barber or hairdresser.

part four

How to Protect Yourself

chapter 13

Get It in Writing

"Get it in writing" is a hackneyed phrase heard countless times from childhood on. Nonetheless, it still works, especially when you're up against your local garage.

Consider the proud owner of a 1970 Mercury Marquis, who went to his dealer for some routine repairs and to get his car's transmission fixed. He had been experiencing trouble with the transmission since he purchased the car but the dealer had never been able to fix it. This time the service manager promised to fix it once and for all—the next time he came in.

This bothered the owner because his warranty was about to expire. Don't worry, comforted the service manager; since the problem had been brought to his attention before the warranty ran out, the transmission would be properly adjusted and repaired without charge when the needed part came in.

The owner was a trusting soul. He went home and returned two weeks later when the elusive part came in. The repair was made, the new Mercury was finally able to go both forward and backward, and the car owner was happy—until he was handed a bill. In addition to being charged $60 for the transmission repair, he was socked with charges for new shock absorbers, ball joints, idler arm, and a front-end alignment—none of which he needed and none of which he asked for.

This tale, sad though it may be, is not at all unusual. The same scenario occurs countless times every day and it poses the same questions. Can the car owner hold the service manager to his promise on the warranty? What about the extra repairs—does he have to pay even though he did not request them? Can he get his car back without paying at all?

The answers to these questions don't paint a bright picture. But you may have more rights than you think you have, and we'll get to those shortly. Often such problems can be avoided if you first make sure to get everything down on paper.

Few people would consent to any arrangements with a real estate broker, a contractor, or a landscaper without distilling their agreement to writing. Somehow, the sight of all those tools and disassembled automobiles prompts agreements between a mechanic and a customer with nothing but a signature even though substantial amounts of money are involved. Verbal agreements are not any more memorable because they were made under a grease rack, as you could learn from many a car owner appearing in court with nothing but a repair order filled in by the mechanic.

Having in writing what went on between you and the mechanic could avoid many a dispute and could stand you in good stead in the event there is one. Memories tend to fade. Though few people willingly perjure themselves, it is only human to remember things the way we wish they had happened rather than the way they did.

Kinds of Agreements

When purchasing auto repairs, a written agreement is especially important to protect yourself against faulty work or deception in the following categories:

The estimate: Getting a written estimate is about the best protection you can have against a padded bill, and it is not at all difficult for the mechanic to give you one. The flat-rate book, explained in greater detail in chapter 14, indicates the exact number of hours a particular job will take and what parts will have to be used. From that, the mechanic should be able to tell you exactly what your bill will be.

Warranty promises: If you are so fortunate as to have extracted a promise from your dealer beyond those of the warranty, better get him to put it in writing. This is particularly true when the dealer, who has been putting off certain warranty-covered repairs for one reason or another, finally tells you: "Although your warranty coverage will be over, I'll make the repairs next time you come in." When you return and remind him of his agreement he has conveniently forgotten or changed his mind. You stand a better chance of jogging his memory if you have his promise on paper. Besides, a written warranty modification is enforceable in court and your dealer will be aware of that.

The guarantee: If you are getting your car repaired and the garage says there will be a ninety-day guarantee, get in writing exactly what is guaranteed. Usually, it will be only the parts, which the garage already has a guarantee on from the manufacturer. Your guarantee should include the second labor charge; you should not have to pay twice because the garage installed a defective part or installed a good part improperly.

This guarantee of ninety days, whether it covers parts and labor or only parts, is generally not on the repair order. Get the mechanic to write it on the repair order, or on a separate piece of paper referable to the repair order, and sign it.

You can also protect yourself by knowing what written "guarantees" really mean.

When a guarantee is used as part of an advertising gimmick, be especially cautious. Guarantees such as "good for the life of your car," "25 percent off labor and parts when work is done in our garage," and the fifty-fifty-thirty guarantee where the mechanic promises to pay half the cost of replacement if his work goes sour within thirty days are usually worthless whether they are in writing or not.

The FTC censured Midas for guaranteeing its mufflers for the life of your car. What Midas's guarantee really meant was for as long as you own the car and are willing to pay a service charge to have a new muffler installed and to pay for the extras—such as clamps, hangers, and brackets—that go with the muffler. The Midas guarantee covers about 12 percent of the cost of most replacement jobs. The "25 percent off labor and parts when the work is done in our garage" means 25 percent off the highest price they can get away with. Such a guarantee also insures that you will be back to their garage so they can get another crack at your business.

The fifty-fifty-thirty guarantee is the tool of the

used-car dealer. If something goes wrong and he can't stall you beyond the thirty-day period, he will jack up the price of the repair so that the half you pay is the total cost plus a profit for him.

One of the ruses used by a nationally franchised brake center to get around the guarantee is to blame the faulty repair on another part of the car. For instance, you go in for the $19.95 brake special with a lifetime guarantee. A few months later, all is not well with the brakes and you go back, guarantee in hand. You may well be told that the brake special included adjustments and new linings but not new brake fluid and whatever it is that is wrong with your brakes now.

Don't buy a repair job because it is guaranteed unless you know what the guarantee covers—and what it doesn't cover.

The Mechanic's Lien

That piece of paper you sign when you leave your car for repairs in the morning carries a lot of clout. It's not just a work order, as it is often called. It is actually a mechanic's lien which entitles the garage to keep your car until you pay, and the garage doesn't even have to prove that the charges are legitimate. If you refuse to pay, the garage can sell your car for the cost of repairs and keep the money. As an added touch of larceny, the mechanic often sells the car to himself for the amount of the repair bill—seldom more than a few hundred dollars. He then turns around and resells the car at the going price, a hefty profit for him.

This may sound harsh and, as it operates today, it

is. Back in the early days of the automobile, when garages and cars were small, the mechanic felt he had to protect himself from the unscrupulous car owner who might leave his car for repairs, return to pick it up, and drive off without paying. The mechanic discovered that repairing a car was like healing the sick: you can't take back what you've done, even if you don't get paid for it. The healed body and the repaired car are both mobile.

Undoing what had been done—disconnecting wires, loosening bolts, draining out clean oil and putting back the sludge—didn't seem to be a sensible answer. So ingenious legal minds came up with the mechanic's lien; that is, give the mechanic who makes improvements on your car a lien on it—the car is his to sell unless you pay for the repairs.

As early as 1914, the Arkansas Court of Appeal upheld the mechanic's lien. The lien, which existed at common law on personal property for the value of repairs made thereto, was extended to the labor and material which had been expended and used in repairing an automobile. In extending the personal property lien, the Arkansas court explained:

Automobiles are a species of vehicles which was unknown at common law but little doubt can be entertained that, in the absence of a statute, wheelwrights and mechanics would be entitled to a lien on the automobile.

Today most states have enacted laws which makes the common law lien a statutory right.

It is doubtful whether such a presumption in favor of the mechanic is needed today. The mechanic's lien, like the running board and the crank, may have been needed by the infant automobile industry in the early

1900s. Few would contend today that General Motors needs to be protected from its customers. Yet, as the law reads now, the mechanic need only assert a claim for a certain amount of money; if not paid, he can sell your car.

The mechanic's lien is a devastating weapon only because the mechanic can enforce his claim by selling your car without going to court. There is, however, one sure defense. You are safe from a mechanic's lien if you do not own your car outright. If you are still paying on your car under a conditional sales contract, the mechanic cannot sell your car because he must provide the new owner with a certificate of title to the automobile which he cannot obtain unless his lien was prior in time to the notation on the certificate of title. In every case, the company that financed the purchase of your car is prior in time.

Feisty consumer groups and activist lawyers are challenging the constitutionality of the mechanic's lien in a number of states. They won in Texas where the right to sell a person's property even with a lien on it without a court hearing was declared unconstitutional.

The law reform unit of the Neighborhood Legal Services programs, which is bringing the suits, is confident that other states will follow Texas's lead.

While the law slowly changes, you have to protect yourself. Some disgruntled car owners are challenging the lien on their own by taking their car back without paying or writing a check and then stopping payment.

Strictly speaking, there are some legal problems in resorting to such tactics. When a mechanic has a lien on a car he does have the right to sell it, even to himself, for the cost of the repairs. As such the lien is a very valuable property right, the deprivation of which the law punishes. Technically, the mechanic could charge you with larceny.

In practice, however, this has never been the case. Pressing criminal charges would not get the mechanic's bill paid. To get his money, he would still have to file a claim in civil court and prove that the repairs and charges were legitimate. If he were foolish enough to press criminal charges, you would have a complete defense since there was a bona fide dispute over whether the charges were actually due.

Frequently, however, consumers do stop payment on a check as a way to avoid paying for faulty, unordered, or unreceived repairs. Most people feel, and understandably so, that they should not have to pay for something they did not get. Customers are also aware that once the bill is paid, the chances diminish substantially of getting the wrong righted voluntarily. And, since it is human nature to avoid legal battles, the person who gets his money can feel fairly secure that he will not be taken to court over it.

In fact, some reformed mechanics will admit that they keyed their larceny to a legal scale of anger. They carefully avoided cheating an individual out of a large sum of money—that is, a sum large enough to interest a lawyer. They presumed, usually quite accurately, that few individuals bilked out of $100 will spend $200 on a lawyer to get it back. It is only the rare individual—whose bankroll matches his anger—who will go to such an expense. (Small claims court is changing this to some extent; see chapter 18.)

With all this in mind, you may decide to stop payment on that check you wrote at the garage until you and your mechanic come to terms on how much it should be and whether the car is fixed properly. Technically, you may be guilty of false pretenses. Practically speaking, you have just turned the tables so that the mechanic has to explain the charges, redo his work, or otherwise justify his claim. The existence of a bona fide dispute is equally effective as a defense against false pretenses.

Before stopping payment, make sure you have sufficient funds in your bank account to cover the check. Otherwise, you may be accused of writing a bad check.

Stopping payment on a check for a used car or new car purchased on an installment plan raises additional problems. In most cases, the note you sign for the purchase of a car is turned over to a finance company or a bank, which becomes a "holder in due course." As such, the finance company is absolutely entitled to payment even if the car you bought is falling apart. When defects in a new or used car are the reason you want to stop payment on a check, check with a lawyer first.

The FTC is trying to abolish the "holder in due course" doctrine, an antiquated credit law that allows both the retailer and the creditor to duck any responsibility for legitimate consumer complaints. About a dozen states already have eliminated the doctrine altogether, and many more have abolished or restricted it in the case of car sales. Some of the latter states, however, require that you raise your complaints within a certain time after purchasing the car, usually ten to thirty days. Check with the local office of your state attorney general to find out the requirements in your state.

Advance protection: To avoid the big headache of returning to pick up your car and finding extra work done, take some extra precautions when signing the repair order. There are a few ways in which you can modify the order so that the honest mechanic is assured of payment but you are protected from his less scrupulous colleagues.

—Cross out the blank lines on the order. Do this after all the work to be done and all the parts to be used are filled in. If you don't take this precaution, it's like handing the mechanic a blank check.

—Initial the repairs. After the line items are filled in, go back and initial each item. Then add "for repairs initialed hereunder" to the paragraph that appears just above where you sign your name. This paragraph usually includes acknowledgment of a mechanic's lien and reads roughly as follows: "I hereby authorize the repair work hereinafter set forth to be done along with the necessary material, and hereby grant you and/or your employees permission to operate the car or truck herein described on streets, highways or elsewhere for the purpose of testing and/or inspection. An express mechanic's lien is hereby acknowledged on above car or truck to secure the amount of repairs thereto." You would delete the word "thereto" and add "initialed hereunder."

—Get an estimate. Before you sign the repair order, have the service writer look up the charges in the flat-rate manual, which 90 percent of the garages use. Have the amounts filled in before you sign.

These three steps protect you from the chief abuses of overcharging and overfixing. They might also cause you some extra inconvenience, however. A mechanic may discover another item which needs fixing once he starts working on your car, one which you did not authorize on the order. If he calls you and then goes ahead with the repair, he takes the chance of non-payment since he lacks a lien on the added repairs. He might even choose to wait for a new authorization before doing the work.

But that is a minor risk when you consider what a crafty mechanic can do with all those blank spaces. Here is a scene that has been repeated often:

An owner takes his car to a dealer for "winterizing" —that Madison Avenue slogan for flushing and draining the cooling system and filling it with a new solution. The mechanic probably can't beat the time allotted for that job, since he has to wait for the system to drain several times. But he could be using that dead time to turn a tidy profit by changing spark plugs, points, and condenser, putting on a new fan belt, or performing a number of other quick fixes. Later when he hands you the bill, he will argue that the extra work was needed. And you are caught with a bill three times larger than you planned, all because you neglected to cross out those empty spaces and initial the winterizing job.

The carefully filled-in repair order also serves as a warning to the mechanic. You may not know a condenser from a differential, but the garageman knows from your repair order that you won't go down without a fight. If a mechanic is prone to gouging customers, he is likely to wait for one that looks less troublesome than you.

chapter 14 ───────────────────

Flat Rates and Lofty Charges

To protect yourself from being overcharged for repairs, you need to know how repair charges are figured. Crossing out blanks and initialing repair items on a repair order may seem to be overkill. But you are not being overcautious when you consider the system under which mechanics work, a system that encourages the overcharging and overfixing you must be on guard against.

All these warnings may make every mechanic sound like Attila the Hun. In fairness to a profession under fire, the questionable tactics some use to earn an extra buck are not all of their own making. Mechanics, too, sometimes are victims of the system.

Mechanics work under a pay system that rewards fast and, consequently, sloppy work in a search for profits. Mechanics generally are not paid straight salary according to how many years they have been in the business, how much training they have, or their skill. Instead, they work on a commission, getting about 40 percent of the take on a particular job. In large garages and dealerships, where there is a service writer and parts manager who also work on commission, there is a triple-barreled effort to use as many parts and as much time on a particular car as the market allows.

For instance, you drive your slightly battered 1969 Plymouth Valiant into a dealer's garage to get a new fan belt. The service writer writes it up. You sign. As it stands, the mechanic will get 40 percent of the bill, the service manager 10 percent and the parts manager 10 percent (the service manager and the parts manager get the commission in addition to a straight salary) of a bill for about $6. If the mechanic can find additional work he can do, he can up the total on the repair order and everybody's take increases.

The same incentive applies to the service manager who can write up more repairs than are necessary. The service manager is usually chosen for his skills as a salesman rather than as a mechanic (often he is not a mechanic at all). If he can get you to leave your car without deciding what needs to be done, or sign a repair order with vaguely worded items like "tune-up," his day will be successful. He can later combine his sales skills with the mechanic's technical knowledge and take you for a real ride. (The commission system also explains why car dealer employees and mechanics aren't interested in wasting their time on warranty repairs.)

The commission system is further complicated by the mechanic's failure to unionize. His hourly rate in an area or region is always substantially below that paid other technicians, such as airplane mechanics, who have organized. In fact, manufacturers set the labor rate for their dealers by surveying the local area and then setting the mechanic's wage below that of the unionized trades.

Ford now has a practice of allowing for escalation of labor rates of dealers in a given market area in line with figures of mechanics' wages reported by the Bureau of Labor Statistics, a system which puts mechanics employed by the auto industry in the same class as mechanics employed by the airline and appliance industries.

The Flat-Rate Manual

The repair-charging game also is stacked against the customer by the way the number of hours for which a mechanic will be paid are computed, called the flat-rate system.

The flat-rate system is only a slight improvement on the old piecework concept under which sweatshop seamstresses were paid by the number of shirts they could finish in a sixteen-hour day. Under the flat-rate system, the customer is charged not for the amount of time actually spent repairing his car, but for the amount of time a reference book—known as the flat-rate manual—says the repairs should have taken. For example, replacing the brake linings takes 1.2 hours and overhauling a carburetor takes 3.5 hours, according to one flat-rate manual.

Auto manufacturers devised the system to try to bring some sort of order and quality of repair to the service departments. A brake job is a brake job is a brake job, say the auto manufacturers, and it shouldn't cost more to have one mechanic work on your car than another.

But the flat-rate concept encourages abuse in two ways. First, the mechanic knows when he begins to replace, say, the fuel pump that he will only be paid for forty-eight minutes' worth of work. If a problem crops up and the repair takes an hour and a half, he still gets paid for only forty-eight minutes. Thus, he tends to rush through the job to avoid losing money.

Second, since he is continually racing the clock, the mechanic is also encouraged to replace a part rather than repair it. Generators often fail because the brushes wear out. In the military, where time and cheap labor are plentiful, electricians spend countless hours replacing generator brushes. It is considered routine maintenance and is much more economical than replacing the entire generator. But the mechanic working on your car can cut his time in half by simply replacing the entire generator rather than taking extra minutes to disassemble the old part and make the necessary repair. The customer saves a bit on labor time but pays far more in the long run for a new part that wasn't necessary.

The flat-rate system also leads to a pitch-till-you-win approach to car repairs, particularly in the hands of a slow but competent mechanic. He cannot afford to spend extra minutes diagnosing the problem or troubleshooting on the car owner's behalf. He must do something quickly, or he won't get paid. So, first he replaces the spark plugs. If that doesn't do the trick he installs new points and a condenser. The car still isn't running right so in goes a new distributor. Your car may eventually get fixed, but you end up paying for a bushel of unneeded parts.

Most mechanics race the flat-rate clock. Many can log twenty flat-rate hours in an eight-hour day by barreling through their jobs. The manuals list a brake job at 2.3 flat-rate hours. The mechanic, by cutting corners, can do two brake jobs in two hours and get paid for 4.6 hours' work. The customer still pays for

2.3 hours' labor while the mechanic has spent only one hour on his car.

In addition to all the other problems with the flat-rate system, there is more than one flat-rate manual in use. Each of the manufacturers puts out his own. Then there are several others put out by independent automotive publishers which are used by most independent garages and gas stations. The independent's flat-rate manual allows more time for each job than the manufacturer's does. The reason: the manufacturer must reimburse the dealer for warranty work. Therefore, he skimps on the time to save himself money.

On the other hand, flat-rate times in the Chilton manual, the one often used by nondealers, are computed without the use of power tools. Since most garages use power tools, it's no trick for a mechanic to beat the book on certain repairs—but still charge you for the allotted time. At Senator Hart's hearings, Chilton defended this on the ground that a businessman-mechanic "cannot simply charge a lower rate and penalize himself for his investment and his efficiency."

Flat-rate proponents say the consumer is protected under this system. If a mechanic spends longer than the allotted time fixing your car, you are still only charged the book time, they argue. This seldom occurs in practice, however. If the mechanic beats the book time, you are still charged the listed flat-rate hours. If he goes over, you pay the actual time consumed, not the flat-rate time.

Needed Reforms

The alternative to flat rates is simple: Pay the mechanic a fixed salary. Then he can ignore the clock and devote his attention to fixing your car. Picture the number of buildings that would be falling down if the construction worker were paid by the number of nails he pounded in per day.

A salaried mechanic faced with a stalling vehicle, unconcerned with how many "jobs" he writes up for you, might test the electric system, fuss with the throttle linkage, and inspect the fuel pump. He might end up cleaning the carburetor and replacing a 35-cent part. Most motorists would be happy to pay the mechanic $10 for an hour's worth of labor plus the 35-cent part, rather than shelling out money for plugs, points, condenser, and distributor to a mechanic who is trying to log extra flat-rate hours.

There is not much you can do to protect yourself against the abuses that result from the use of the flat-rate system—inadequate diagnosis, rapid repairs, spurious repairs, and insubstantial testing of repairs made. This is because all dealers and many garages use it. The best protection, of course, is to shop around for the garage that pays its mechanics straight salaries. You are very likely to get substantially better repairs from that garage. If you can't find one, or don't have the time to shop, do this:

—Ask if the shop uses the flat-rate system to compute its labor charge. If the answer is yes, ask to see the flat-rate manual from which the mechanic computes his times. If it is an independent garage, expect to be shown Chilton's If it is a dealership, expect to be shown the manufacturer's flat-rate book. Have the mechanic show you the job as it is listed in the book.

—When you get your car fixed at a dealership, he should be using his manufacturer's flat-rate book. If, for example, a mechanic at a Ford dealership shows you a Chilton manual, question him, especially if your car is being repaired under warranty The manufacturer requires that the dealer use his book and no other. Some dealers pay their mechanics by the manufacturer's book and charge the customers by Chilton's, making extra on the labor charge which they do not have to divvy with the mechanic.

—When caught charging more flat-rate hours than they should, a garage may say that more than one mechanic worked on your car, so they doubled the time. Seldom can two mechanics work on one item on your car. Do not accept this excuse.

—A discrepancy between your bill and the time listed in the flat-rate manual provides an excellent case for small claims court. You need no further documentation of your claim of excessive charges. Pay if you must. If by check, add the words "without prejudice to rights." * If in cash, have the garage sign the bill to which you have added the words "without prejudice to rights."

Again, be sure you take advantage of the only asset of the flat-rate system. Since the labor charge is computed not by the amount of time it will take the mechanic to fix your car but by the amount of time

---

* *Without prejudice to rights:* that as between the two parties, the payment of money by one and its receipt by the other admits nothing; that their dispute shall be open to settlement by legal controversy as if the money had not been paid.

the book says it should take, the mechanic can give you an exact price before you leave the garage. Get one before you sign the order and the mechanic will be less likely to tack on additional repairs.

Many of the flat-rate manuals are available at your local library. If you want to find out how long a repair you had done—or plan to have done—should take under the flat-rate system, you can check the book yourself. The missing variable is the labor rate, which you'll have to find out from the garage. Or you can call a gas station and ask them the time for a particular repair.

How to Get Your Car Fixed for Free; the Recall Campaigns

Everyone talks about cars coming off the assembly line with more and more defects, but not everybody knows there is something he or she can do about some of the defects in his or her own car.

One provision of the 1966 National Traffic and Motor Vehicle Safety Act requires that:

Every manufacturer of motor vehicles shall furnish notification of any defect in any motor vehicle . . . which he determines relates to motor vehicle safety, to the purchaser (where known to the manufacturer) . . . within a reasonable time after such manufacturer has discovered such defect.

This provision of the 1966 law has prompted what is popularly known as the recall campaigns, and it has resulted in the recall of over 31 million vehicles by manufacturers to check for possible safety defects. Such recall campaigns, however, have run into a couple of problems.

For one, many motorists ignore notification warnings from the manufacturers about defects. Part of this is due to apathy. But a great deal of the low response is due to the way the car companies describe the suspected defects. The National Highway Traffic Safety Agency has told the car makers that their recall letters don't warn customers adequately of the safety hazards involved. Many customers, not realizing the safety risk they run, kiss off such letters as a gimmick to get their cars back to the dealer for repairs, the agency said.

(According to Ralph Nader, the safety agency itself is guilty of "negligent inaction" in investigating possible defects and putting pressure on the car companies to mount recall campaigns. The result is that many cars that should be recalled aren't, Mr. Nader contends.)

Another recall problem is that not everybody who is driving a recalled car gets the word. In a survey of 50,000 car owners whose vehicles were the subject of recall campaigns, the Department of Transportation found that nearly 20 percent failed to receive a notice from the manufacturer that their cars might be defective and should be returned to their dealer for a possible repair.

The lack of notification occurs for various reasons, ranging from halfhearted notification efforts by the manufacturers to changes of addresses by customers. Occasionally there are more exotic problems. A Ford executive tells the story of one customer's complaint about a recall letter for a Mustang that he had purchased for his girlfriend. Only trouble was, the letter was sent to the man's home and opened by his wife—who until then knew nothing about either the Mustang or the girlfriend.

If you have either failed to receive or ignored a recall notice put out on your car, you still may be entitled to a free repair. The auto makers generally repair the defects on recalled cars without charge.

(Not all recalled cars have a defect, but the manufacturers usually call back all of those vehicles which it suspects might have a specified flaw.)

The largest single auto recall was announced in December 1971 when General Motors called back nearly 6.7 million Chevrolets for possibly defective motor mounts. With this recall, General Motors broke its own record set on February 25, 1969, when it recalled 5 million cars for throttle and exhaust problems.

General Motors has competition in the recall sweepstakes. Ford recalled 4 million 1971 and 1972 passenger cars for defective shoulder belt connectors. In 1971 it recalled 215,823 Pintos—all of those it had produced to that time—to check for fuel vapors that might ignite and set the engine on fire. The 400,000 or so owners of the racy new Ford Torinos and Montegos had barely gotten their 1972 cars home from the showroom when they learned they had to take them back to get a device installed which would warn them if their weak rear axle bearings were about to give out, causing the rear wheels to fall off. The public outcry against a recall installing a warning device instead of replacing the possibly defective rear axle was so loud that Ford came out two weeks later with another recall announcement—it would put its plants on overtime to manufacture stronger rear axles which would replace the original Torino and Montego rear axles.

The more than 31 million cars recalled since 1965 amount to one out of every three cars produced during that period. Even these giant numbers do not reflect the whole problem. The Department of Transportation can act only when the defect is safety related. Defects which are only irritating, such as misaligned doors, trunks that won't shut, and door handles that come off in your hand go unrecorded.

Nevertheless, it is clear that the way things are going the auto industry one day may be able to claim total recall. The National Highway Traffic Safety Agency reported that the 14 million U.S. and foreign cars recalled for safety-related defects in the twelve months ending June 1972 was the largest number of recalls for any twelve-month period since the National Motor Vehicle Safety Act was adopted in 1966.

It is interesting to note that the recall of more than 12 million of those cars stemmed from government or other nonindustry probes.

Despite the fact that the responsibility for the defects that merit recall rests squarely on the manufacturer, it is the dealer who is saddled with the ensuing repair headaches. GM's response to its record recall for motor mount defects is indicative of its lack of concern for its mistakes and for its dealers. Letters from over 500 buyers poured into the National Highway Traffic Safety Administration complaining that something was causing their cars' accelerators to clamp to the floor, sending the autos on terrifying runaway trips. Pressured by GM not to initiate a recall, the NHTSA issued a "consumer protection bulletin," a watered-down press release which warned that faulty engine mounts in 1965 through 1969 Chevrolets *might* be defective. After further investigation, NHTSA engineers found that the engine mounts were failing because the rubberized compound holding the rubber to the steel plates was not strong enough. When it gave out, the engine lunged to the side, pulling the accelerator wide open and severing the power brake hoses.

Faced with this additional evidence and mounting incidents, GM agreed to notify 6.7 million Chevrolet owners to bring in their vehicles to the dealer for modification of the engine mount. But in a letter to the Department of Transportation, GM still refused to recognize that any of its cars had come off the assembly line with a defect. The company said it was agreeing to the recall only because "it is apparent that as a result of the publicity which has been given to the engine mount issue, there is a great deal of misinformation and misunderstanding on the part of Chevrolet owners which we are anxious to eliminate." Thus, in GM's eyes the problem is not one of quality control but of creeping Naderism and biased journalism.

Despite the official finding of defect, GM is not going to replace the faulty engine mounts. At $33 a shot, the cost would be over $231,000,000. Instead, GM has authorized its dealers to install wire restraints to prevent the engine from spinning when it breaks. In other words, the mount will still be defective; under acceleration the engine can twist off the mount, jam the throttle, and cause the power steering and brakes to fail—*but* for this straplike device designed to catch the falling engine.

The same was obvious in GM's handling of the 1971 Corvair recall. Though the government said finally that because of defective welding, toxic exhaust fumes may seep into the passenger compartment of the 756,000 Corvairs still on the road, GM refused to pay the cost of repairs. The fatal flaw costs $170 to correct—$20 more than the trade-in value of the car today. Since these cars are generally driven by the less affluent and the young it is doubtful they will be repaired unless GM picks up the tab.

GM may get its comeuppance yet. A 1.26 million dollar class action suit has been filed by California Chevrolet owners against GM charging breach of warranty, fraud, and misrepresentation in the engine mount affair. The suit charges that GM failed to make effective repairs on 6.7 million Chevrolets known to be defective and seeks to compel the company to replace rather than just modify the motor mounts. It also asks for one billion dollars in exemplary damages. GM denied the charges.

Attorneys for the estate of one Chevrolet owner who, along with his wife and two other passengers, was killed when his car went out of control on an interstate highway, sued GM, using the engine mount recall as evidence of negligence. They argued that the loosely anchored engine slipped out of place, sending the car across the divider into the path of an oncoming vehicle. The $600,000 settlement, on November 16, 1972, could prove a costly precedent for GM.

The Department of Transportation publishes a report on recall campaigns every three months. These booklets seldom find their way into the newspapers or into your hands. They contain a brief description of the defect, an evaluation of the risk to safety involved, and a statement of the manufacturer's corrective action.

The appendix contains a summary of the 1971 and 1972 major recall campaigns (over 50,000) of the largest American and foreign auto manufacturers. Copies of the complete recall booklets may be obtained from the Superintendent of Documents, Government Printing Office, Washington, D.C. 20402.

Protective Maintenance

Gardeners, it is said, actually enjoy pulling weeds.

Similarly, there are countless car lovers who look forward to spending a full weekend tinkering with their motor machines, doing the routine maintenance that keeps the engine in top shape. But for most of us, maintenance is a bother; even when someone else does the work, it sometimes gets put off. It shouldn't.

Regular visits to a garage are much like regular visits to the dentist, and not only because each can be painful. Visiting a dentist twice a year is supposed to keep down the number of cavities, but too many people wait until the tooth aches. Similarly, changing the oil in your car every 4000 to 6000 miles prevents more costly repairs later on, but too many people wait until the car won't start before seeking help.

Besides preventing bigger repairs later on, keeping a regular maintenance schedule will make you less vulnerable to the mechanic-salesman who, after fiddling under the hood of your car, announces that the spark plugs need replacing. If you have it written down that you replaced the spark plugs just 3000 miles back, you won't be taken in.

Keeping records also helps when more than one person drives the same car. A quick look at the maintenance schedule in the glove compartment can tell you whether or not your co-driver got that last oil change.

If you have found a regular mechanic, you can set up a mutually agreeable maintenance schedule for your car. If your car is still under warranty, follow the schedule in the warranty book. (Remember, you don't have to get routine maintenance done at the dealer.)

Here, immediately following, is a suggested maintenance schedule covering most of the basic upkeep that should be done periodically. These include the following:

Oil change: In most U.S. cars built since the early 1960s, the engine oil needs to be changed every four months or 6000 miles, whichever comes first. Chrysler Corporation says the oil in its cars should be changed every three months or 4000 miles. Older cars and some foreign models generally require oil changes about every 2000 miles. If the type of driving you do involves trailer hauling or if the car is used mainly for short trips, the oil should be changed more frequently. (Ford reverted to 4000-mile oil changes with its 1973 model cars.)

Oil filter: The oil filter should be replaced every other oil change.

Lubrication: A "lube job" used to go together with an oil change like salt and pepper. It usually includes greasing linkages, hinges, latches, and the chassis. It also should include inspection of the upper and lower ball joints as well as inspection of the rear axle assembly for leakage.

On older cars, a lubrication should be performed about every four months. On many newer model U.S. cars, however, such frequent lubrication isn't needed, according to the manufacturers. This is because the joints in the suspension system and steering system are semipermanently lubricated at the factory with a special grease. All that is needed, the car companies say, is an inspection of those joints every six months and a relubrication every three years or 36,000 miles. And some foreign-car makers say their cars never need to be lubricated.

Some mechanics, however, still recommend lubrications every 6000 miles or so. Otherwise, they contend, the ball joints on some cars wear out sooner than they should. Most garages can handle the type of lubrication required on cars with semipermanent lubrication, but some lack the special tools needed to handle the job on some bigger, luxury-type cars. (Check your warranty book. Some warranties require that the car be lubricated only with certain long-life chassis lubricants.)

Engine tune-up: This usually includes replacing (or cleaning) the spark plugs, replacing the points and condenser, adjusting the carburetor and automatic choke, installing a new rotor, adjusting the engine timing, and checking the engine compression. Generally, the garage also tests and fills the battery and cleans the battery cables.

A tune-up generally is needed about every twelve months, or 12,000 to 15,000 miles. This also is a good time to replace the PCV valve.

Safety check: This usually includes inspection of the braking and exhaust systems, cleaning the brake drums and brake linings, lubricating the backing plate, checking rear seals, and checking all lights. When the brake drums are removed, it is a good idea to have the front wheel bearings repacked at the same time.

A safety check should be done every eight to twelve months, more often if you roll up a lot of miles in a shorter time.

Pollution control check: This can be done when you get an oil change every four months or so. It includes checking the positive crankcase ventilation system, cleaning and reoiling the PCV filter, checking and adjusting the distributor points, and checking the PCV valve, which should be replaced every year.

Tire check: Visually inspect tires for normal wear, uneven wear, cuts and tears. You can take a peek yourself every once in a while or have the mechanic check when you get your car's oil changed. Also check to see that the tires are properly inflated. To do so, buy an inexpensive tire gauge; the meters on the air pumps at gas stations are notoriously inaccurate.

Coolant check: Should be done at least every fall along with a check of all hoses. The radiator should be completely flushed every two years.

Automatic transmission fluid: This should be checked every six months to see if the fluid is at the full level or slightly below (but never above the "F" mark). On older cars, the transmission fluid and filter should be replaced every one to two years, or 12,000 to 24,000 miles. On newer cars, the transmission fluid and filter should last the life of the car. Check your owner's manual if you have one; otherwise, you'll have to check at a reliable garage or write the manufacturer to find out which category your car falls in. (Fluid levels in manual transmissions and power steering units also should be checked every six months.)

Air conditioner: If you have one, it should be inspected each spring. This usually includes checking the hoses, adjusting belts, cleaning the condenser, checking the Freon and, if necessary, the compressor, doing a performance test with a thermometer, and checking the controls and adjusting them if needed.

Fuel filter and air filter: Both should be replaced about every two years or 24,000 miles and checked periodically.

part five

How to Get Your Car Fixed Right, or Get Your Money Back

chapter 17 ———————————————

Wearing Down the Garage

Max P.'s problems began when the 1970 Chevy Nova he had purchased new for his son to drive to college had trouble starting. Then the heater wouldn't work. Squeaking brakes competed noisewise with a squealing transmission; and, for a new car, the Nova burned a lot of oil.

With his son's new car and warranty in tow, Mr. P. returned to his dealer's service department. They took the car, made the repairs and presented him with a bill for fixing the brakes and the heater, items the service manager claimed were not under the warranty. Mr. P. paid without argument, glad to have the car fixed.

Two days later, Mr. P.'s son complained that the inside of the car was like an oven and that the brakes were squeaking again. It was another week before the service department could schedule a repair, and this time there wasn't any charge for the additional service. But the inside of the car still was like an oven, and the brakes still were squeaking.

Mr. P. called back the next day. Oddly enough, the service department was booked solid for the next two weeks. The Chevy Nova was scheduled $2\frac{1}{2}$ weeks in the future.

At this point, Mr. P. took things into his own hands.

Instead of waiting $2\frac{1}{2}$ weeks, he drove the car to his dealer the next day and took the service manager for a ride. The service manager claimed not to hear the brakes squeaking, but the perspiration on his brow indicated that he knew the heater was overworking. Although the garage wasn't busy, the service manager asked Mr. P. to come back another time.

But Mr. P. wasn't brushed off so easily. Instead, he began a campaign of phone calls and visits. He called the service manager four times the first day and six times the second. On the third day, he again took his car in. Again he was told the garage was filled. Mr. P. hung around the garage that morning, talking to other customers and relating his sad tale.

The next day, he began calling again. Finally, he got a response. He was told to bring the car in the next morning. This time the service department replaced the heating coil and overhauled the brakes. The car no longer overheated inside, and the brakes no longer squeaked. And Mr. P. did not have to pay for the repairs.

Such tenacity, you might say, goes above and beyond the call of anger. You may be right. By the time Mr. P. adds up the cost of gas for trips back and forth, the time lost from work, the time wasted at work making phone calls and fuming, as well as the all-around wear and tear on his nervous system, it probably would have been cheaper simply to take his business down the street and pay for the whole job again.

But there are two good arguments against caving in. First, by the time you go back to pick up your car the first time, you already have a considerable investment of time and money in the garage where you began. Second, if you immediately throw in the towel and go elsewhere, you may be trading your present problems for a new set of headaches down the street.

Besides, the tolerance for argument at some garages is quite low. A minimum of fighting back from you might yield results. A good first commandment for a disgruntled auto repair customer might be, "Never give up without *some* fight."

If necessary, the tactics used by Mr. P. can be good ones to follow. Hopefully, you won't have to go as far. The battle to get your repair done right or get your money back is often an escalating one. But it usually is not good strategy to declare all-out war until you have to.

General Tips

The first thing to remember is that if you aren't satisfied with a repair, or think you've been duped, register your complaint immediately. Put it off even a few days and the mechanic will think of all kinds of things that could have caused your problem *after* you left the garage.

If the problem isn't adjusted immediately, don't forget to put your complaint in writing. Typically, a mechanic will tell you that the problem you are complaining about is normal after a specific repair and that it will work itself out. If it doesn't, he'll say, bring the car back and we'll fix it right without charge.

When the problem persists and you take the car back, the mechanic probably will have forgotten his promise or may deny that a faulty repair is to blame. You can avoid that possibility by having the garage write your complaint on your receipt, along with any promises they make to check it later. In fact, you should keep a written record of all your car repairs and repair complaints that weren't taken care of properly, especially if your car is under warranty.

If you're lucky, and the garage is reasonable, just voicing a simple complaint may be all you need to get the repair fixed properly, or to get your money back if, for example, you were overcharged. If it isn't, the tactics you may want to consider next will depend partly on the type of garage you are dealing with.

Wearing Down the Dealership

Wearing down the garage is especially time consuming and frustrating if a dealership is causing your problems. The bureaucratic set-up of many of these large outfits can send you around in circles, with the mechanic referring you to the service manager and the service manager referring you to the zone representative (if it is a new car under warranty) or to one of the vice-presidents. Vice-presidents in dealerships are like the vice-president of the United States—long on title but short on authority. Often they are simply senior salesmen who can make deals on the showroom floor. Seldom do they bother themselves with the service department problems.

Once you have registered your complaint with the service manager, the best tactic, usually the only tactic, is to bypass the various functionaries in a dealership and head directly for the president. The service manager's job is to field the day-to-day complaints by getting rid of them. If he were to report the complaints to the official hierarchy, by definition, he wouldn't be doing his job. The president is probably a more adept businessman who can spot trouble.

By heading straight for the top, you identify yourself as someone who is not giving up. Rather than begin on what promises to be a protracted dispute, he or she may settle the problem. The second commandment in the disgruntled customer handbook is not to be apologetic. Remember, you aren't asking for any favors, just what you paid for.

If you can't get anywhere with the dealer-owner, you can try calling or writing the zone manager of the manufacturer. Your owner's manual should list the addresses of zone managers. You can present your case to him and perhaps arrange to have him look at your car and the problems you are complaining about. This is where it may also help to have a written record of your service problems with the dealer. For owners of Ford Motor Company cars, Ford has opened customer service offices in thirty-four major cities to handle complaints about dealer service.

Don't expect any miracles, however. Occasionally, the zone manager will overrule the dealer. More often, he will express a form letter sympathy for your problem but note that, alas, the car dealer is an independent businessman and the manufacturer can't control his repair service. This, of course, is the same independent businessman who must dance to the manufacturer's sales tune or lose his franchise.

Here, for example, is the reply received by a Maryland housewife in response to a two-page letter in which she catalogued over $200 worth of complaints about the new car she purchased from a dealer who was not interested in fixing it. Her letter traveled the corporate circle from the main office of General Motors in Detroit back to the zone dealer who, after expressing his dedication to service, referred her back to the dealer who caused the problems in the first place. The form letter, which varies only slightly from the form letters used by the other major manufacturers, went like this:

We have been requested to acknowledge your letter of recent date addressed to our central office in Detroit, Michigan, because matters of this nature must be handled by this location.

Since Chevrolet and quality Chevrolet dealers attach the greatest importance to the personal attention of Chevrolet owners, we have reviewed your comments. As a result, we have forwarded a copy of your correspondence to your dealer so that he or his qualified representative can contact you. . . .

If, perchance, you do win a concession from the dealer or car company, don't let your guard down. The dealer, for example, may agree to do some warranty work and then give your car the "sunshine" treatment. This means that after you drive your car to the dealer and go on about your business, the dealership simply leaves your car out in the sunlight all day right where you parked it and then tells you the free warranty repairs were made when you come to pick the car up.

A good idea, when you leave your car for any warranty repairs, is to mark down the odometer reading to the tenth of a mile, or mark your tires, and then check when you return to see if the car has been moved.

If you strike out with both the dealer and the zone

manager, you can write a letter to the car manufacturer. But, again, don't expect this to generate much action either. What kind of letter to write, and who to send it to, are subjects discussed more fully later in this chapter.

Wearing Down the Independent Garage

With an independent repair shop, you aren't as likely to get as much of a runaround. Hopefully, you won't get much resistance in the first place. As mentioned before, the service at independent garages is much more personal and therefore complaints are much easier to work out. Also, the independent has a much greater stake in the outcome. He can't risk a bad press from his customers whom he depends on for repeat business and advertisements.

Chances are, the owner will be on hand, so getting to someone who can make a decision is a simple matter. If the owner does prove to be stubborn about a legitimate complaint, he may be susceptible to the following prods:

—Write a letter to the local licensing board. Mechanics aren't licensed but their shops are. The garage can't operate without such a permit and the permit can be revoked in most cities by the licensing board if a number of complaints are lodged against a business and found to be valid. Most independent businessmen don't want to risk an investigation by the city and will work out the dispute with you so that the complaint will be taken off their record.

—Come back to the garage for the second time when you know many of his customers will be coming to pick up their cars, usually around five o'clock. You will find a ready-made audience in the waiting area, and it can more easily identify with your problem than the garage owner's. He may want to put an end to the dispute right there—publicly—so that he does not get a bad reputation.

—Write a letter to his association—usually the Independent Garage Owners of America—a group with strong sanctions against members who do not live up to their code of ethics.

Wearing Down the Franchised Specialty Shop

If your problem is with one of the franchised specialty shops, or with a gas station, you can start by tracking down the owner and appealing to him as an independent businessman, which he is in some respects. Indeed, some of the tactics that apply to independent garages also apply to local franchised garages and service stations. If these tactics don't work, an added weapon here is that you can take your complaint to the oil company or franchiser that controls the local outlet.

When a franchised specialty shop is involved, you should also write the Federal Trade Commission, which has been investigating franchisers and their modes of doing business. Those franchisers who have been the subject of FTC complaints in the past are especially sensitive to consumer complaint letters when they know a copy has been sent to the FTC.

Drastic Measures

No matter what type of garage is involved, if the usual tactics don't work the car owner can turn to the more elaborate attack, such as the persistent phone calls and visits used by Mr. P. Some frustrated car owners have resorted to even more dramatic ploys to get publicity, if not always a cure, for their car repair ills.

They include:

—Eddie Campos, whose 1970 Lincoln boasts a five-foot lemon tree protruding through a hole whacked in the roof. Mr. Campos doused his car with gasoline and set it afire outside the Ford plant in Whittier, California. The burned-out hulk is now parked in front of Mr. Campos's plastering business with a tree growing out of its middle and a sign that says "If it's lemons you are going to buy, you might as well grow your own." Mr. Campos's vendetta against Ford began when he brought the car home and his wife took it for a drive. When she returned and pulled the key from the ignition, the whole assembly came with it. The $6500 car went downhill from there.

—Jack Boswell, a Crystal Bay, Nevada, shuttle-bus operator, took his Ford vehicle frustrations out against Ford by running ads in the local paper offering to help any other U.F.O. (Unhappy Ford Owner) press legitimate complaints of over $1000 against Ford. Mr. Boswell reported that responses soon amounted to nearly $750,000 in damage claims, either as joint complaint suits or class action suits. Meanwhile, Mr.

Boswell, who is president of Sitzmark Shuttle System, Inc., has labeled his buses with the phrase: *"Ford is a four letter word."*

—James Hammond, who, after repeated attempts to get his 1970 Toyota fixed, burned it at the Shaefer and Strohmenger dealership in Baltimore, the scene of his many attempts to get service. Mr. Hammond finally got a response from the dealership, but he is now concentrating on his consumer organization which is pressuring area dealerships through picketing, complaint handling, and organization.

Such extreme tactics aren't necessarily recommended, but they show just how far some frustrated car owners are willing to go. Indeed, Mr. Hammond's plight won the sympathy of a Baltimore judge who let him off on probation without a verdict after he was charged with a disorderly conduct charge stemming from his car burning. "Instead of protesting the war, he protested against what he called inferior workmanship. Apparently this thinking had built up in him until he had a cause," the judge was quoted by Associated Press.

The Complaint Letter

A key weapon in any dissatisfied consumer's arsenal is a good complaint letter. Much depends on how the letter is written and who gets it.

The best kind of letter to write is a factual, well-ordered account of what happened to cause your dissatisfaction. It is not necessary to be apologetic—"I don't want to seem like a crank, but. . . ." On the other hand, making threats—"If you don't fix my car I'll fix your wagon"—is just as bad.

A little controlled indignation is all right, but facts are most important. And if you still have a sense of humor left, the right blend of wit and sarcasm sometimes will get your letter the attention that a more routine letter would not.

Your letter should contain the following information:

—Your name, address, and telephone number.

—The name of the garage and its location.

—Your make of car and model year (and warranty number if it is a warranty complaint).

—A description of what took place on what dates and what has been done to resolve the complaint.

—A brief total of how much the dispute has cost you in money, time lost from work, cabs, buses, and getting repairs elsewhere.

—Copies of repair orders and other letters or written material between you and the garage.

Then, without too much editorializing, you should describe the conduct of the person you were dealing with. This could include how your complaint was received, the person's willingness to talk the problem through, and his effort to solve the problem. Even if the latter effort was nil, it still doesn't pay to go into a personalized harangue. As an assistant attorney in a U.S. attorney's office comments: "The more personal criticism the letter contains, the less likely it is that it will be taken seriously. Besides, it usually contains less of the necessary information."

Who the letter goes to is important. If it is to a company, the complaint should be addressed to the head man, even though he isn't likely to see it himself. At smaller companies, the president may get the letter and prompt some action on your behalf if you make a good case.

You should also send copies to government agencies or consumer groups that might be able to help you. The notation that copies are being sent to others may prod the company to take some action in order to avoid bad publicity. For the latter reason, you should also call or write the action line column of your local newspaper, if it has one. Such columns are especially effective against local companies.

Just to whom you should send copies of your complaint letter depends on your individual grievance. The alternatives are discussed more fully in the following sections. Just remember to keep one copy of your letter for your own records.

Private Companies and Organizations: You sometimes can get more attention from your complaint letter if you write directly to the head of the company involved. If it is a local company, you can usually find out the head person's name by calling the concern. For national companies, go to the library and ask for a copy of either *Poor's Register of Corporations, Directors and Executives* or *Moody's Industrial Manual*. Both publications list the addresses of major companies and the names of their top officers.

A sampling of the private companies and organizations you might want to write to with your complaint is given in appendix 3.

"Your Man in Detroit"

The U.S. auto manufacturers have launched, with much ballyhoo, new programs designed to handle consumer complaints. Indeed, television watchers might believe the warranty coverage has been extended or that warranty service is getting better. In an effort to out-consumer one another, the auto companies are in the midst of advertising campaigns that have traded the hard-sell of youth, sex, and power for the softer sell of contrition, understanding, and empathy.

In 1971 Ford launched its "We Listen Better" campaign which admitted the consumer had something to complain about and contended that Ford was trying harder than anyone else to do something about it. The campaign was backed by the same old twelve-month or 12,000 mile warranty and no new consumer remedies. Its 1973 warranty is slightly better. As was the case last year, the company repairs factory defects for the first year and performs maintenance work such as wheel balancing and alignment, carburetor, distributor, valve and transmission adjustments during the first 90 days. Now Ford also offers a written "quality guarantee" of 90 days or 4000 miles on any servicing by its dealers. Ford is also going to have customers fill out score cards on service and will award bonuses to the mechanics with the highest scores. Ford still will not provide a "loaner" car on overnight repairs nor will it handle consumer complaints from corporate headquarters. Ford allows owners to call the company free but only to get the address of the nearest Ford customer service office.

General Motors kept its same warranty but heavily advertised a direct toll-free telephone hotline to its Detroit headquarters permitting General Motors car owners to gripe directly to the people who created their problems. The customer is then referred back to the nearest General Motors customer relations office. General Motors plans no changes in its warranty for 1973.

Chrysler kept the standard twelve-month, 12,000-mile warranty for 1972 with one addition. It named one of its vice-presidents, Byron Nichols, as "Your Man in Detroit." Besides lending status to the customer relations department, Mr. Nichols was supposed to expedite complaints within three days.

He certainly wasn't of any help at all to a woman from Amherst, Massachusetts, who wrote to him when her 1971 Chrysler began to disintegrate. First, an oil leak developed. Then the temperature gauge broke, a piece of metal fell off the clutch, and, finally, the car broke down on Grand Central Parkway in New York and had to be towed.

In desperation she wrote the Chrysler executive: "Can you help me, Mr. Nichols? Will you live up to the promises you made in your ads?"

The answer apparently is no. After waiting for two weeks to hear from Mr. Nichols, the customer called Detroit. Mr. Nichols was unavailable, but she was politely told that her complaint had been processed—it had been sent back to Chrysler's zone office in Natick, Massachusetts, and she should hear from them in five days. However, she was given the phone number of the zone office in case they didn't call.

They didn't. Several phone calls later, she was told in effect that lemons do happen.

The Center for Auto Safety, alarmed by the 250 letters it received complaining about Byron Nichols, decided to check for itself on this phantom consumer ombudsman. It sent thirteen of these complaints to Mr. Nichols asking him to write back to the center after he had helped out the dissatisfied Chrysler owners. After a long delay he replied, but not with the information requested. He said that he had indeed helped the car owners but he could not say how because it was company policy to keep such information secret. The center then wrote to the thirteen Chrysler owners and found that Mr. Nichols had nothing to report because he had done nothing. When the center queried Mr. Nichols again on just what being "Your Man in Detroit" entailed and whether there really was anything he could do for the unhappy customers, he sent back a pile of speeches he had given over the past year. The center countered by filing a complaint with the Federal Trade Commission alleging that Chrysler's "Man in Detroit" was no man at all but just a deception foisted on the American car buyer. The deceptive trade practice complaint, as it is called, is now being investigated by the Federal Trade Commission. Meanwhile, Chrysler has taken Byron Nichols off the air and put him in pamphlet form into the glove compartments of all new Chryslers, awaiting the FTC ruling.

Despite claims of new concern about customer complaints, Ford, General Motors, and Chrysler continue the old pass-the-buck routine of shuffling gripes back to the dealer against whom the complaint was originally filed. In short, the Big Three auto makers claim to be listening better, but their dealers don't seem to be repairing any better. American Motors seems to be taking its conversion to consumerism more seriously. In October 1971, American announced its "Buyer Protection Plan," which promises to pay for the repair or replacement of any parts in its 1972 models that are defective.

"If anything goes wrong with one of our '72's, we'll fix it free. Anything," American Motors proclaimed in full-page ads. That's strong language coming from an auto maker; warranties in the past have been purposely designed more to protect the auto manufacturer from having to fix its defective cars than to protect its customers from shoddy workmanship and parts. What's more, American Motors promises that most dealers will kick in a loaner car if the customer's auto has to be left overnight for repairs.

To carry out such a warranty, American will have to go a long way toward cleaning up its own house. Quality control is a major headache for all car makers and, along with recalcitrant dealers, accounts for much of the dismal warranty service of the past. But American Motors claims it has licked that problem. Every 1973 car (not just one in 50) will be checked and road-tested before being delivered. Then the dealer signs a checklist attesting to the fact that all thirty-two predelivery inspections were made. American also tosses in a direct toll-free line to Detroit, which is novel in that you get the name and telephone number of a warm body in Detroit who is individually responsible for tending to any problems you might have with your new car. It has even beefed up its protection on 1973 models with "trip interruption protection"— if an owner's car breaks down more than 100 miles from home and must undergo repairs covered by the warranty, the company will pay the owner for his food and lodging expenses up to $150.

The program seems to be paying off. Employment at American Motors plants increased 9 percent during the 1972 model year, "reflecting increased production and sales."

The new programs are encouraging in that they indicate that Detroit at last is willing to admit that car owners sometimes do have legitimate complaints. But initial indications are that—with the possible exception of American Motors—the much promoted concern programs amount to little more than glorified versions of the traditional runaround.

The Better Business Bureau

Among private, complaint-handling organizations, the best known is probably the Better Business Bureau. When consumers were asked in a survey where they would go for help if cheated by a merchant, the BBB was the agency most often cited by the minority who had even an idea of where they would go for professional help. Most consumers think the bureau is an organization that gives recommendations and endorsements, passes judgment on the qualifications of merchants and recovers money from unscrupulous businessmen.

For the most part, these consumers are misinformed. The BBB is an independent agency of dues-paying businessmen. Its main purpose is to protect its members and keep fly-by-nighters out of town. The BBB's programs include answering inquiries from the public concerning the reliability of companies with which they plan to do business. In some cities, the caller is given a stock reply, "The business cooperates with us." Translation: They pay dues.

In short, don't depend too much on the local BBB to inform you candidly of complaints against member companies, or to intercede on your behalf. There are some exceptions—the BBB office in St. Louis, for one, has earned a strong consumer-protector reputation—but the overall record is spotty. A group of businessmen concerned about this image is trying to reorganize the BBB through its national office. Any complaints you send to your local BBB should also be sent to the Council of Better Business Bureaus in Washington, D.C.

The address of the Better Business Bureau and those of other private organizations you might want to write to are given in appendix 3.

Federal Agencies

You also should send copies of your complaint letter to one or more of the various federal agencies that oversee programs to help consumer affairs:

—The White House Office of Consumer Affairs
—The Consumer Protection Agency
—The Federal Trade Commission
—Senator Hart's Senate Subcommittee on Antitrust and Monopoly
—The National Highway Traffic Safety Administration

Most of these federal offices can't do much to help you personally. At best, they can use the information you provide them with in preparing legislation, enforcing existing laws, and undertaking investigations. The massive probe of AAMCO Transmission by the FTC was instigated in part by consumer complaints. You can also file a complaint at a local FTC office, which has been given increased authority to work with local protection agencies to protect consumers.

The National Highway Traffic Safety Administration of the Department of Transportation is charged with enforcing the National Traffic and Motor Vehicle Safety Act of 1966. The NHTSA uses consumer letters to assist its defects division in deciding when a recall campaign should be sought. In one case, a single complaint letter to the agency from a Buick owner with a sticking accelerator resulted in a recall of 12,000 1970 Buick Skylarks for replacement of "possibly kinked" throttle cables. GM's recall of 6.6 million Chevrolets to replace defective motor mounts —the biggest auto recall yet—stemmed from owners' letters to the NHTSA, Ralph Nader, and *Detroit News* auto-writer Bob Irvin.

One place where you might get some help with your complaint is the White House Office of Consumer Affairs. In 1969, Virginia Knauer, President Nixon's consumer adviser and director of the Consumer Affairs Office, began a policy of forwarding consumer complaint letters to the manufacturers involved, along with a letter from her on White House stationery urging that the company look into the matter. This sometimes helps since most companies are interested in presenting a good face to the White House.

The White House Office of Consumer Affairs also will handle consumer complaints. You can strengthen its role as a spokesman for consumers by sending your complaint letters there.

Senator Hart's subcommittee, which held hearings on the auto repair industry over three years would be interested in receiving a copy of any complaint. Senator Hart has sponsored legislation that would upgrade the industry's mechanics and provide for a nationwide network of diagnostic and inspection centers. He needs all the support by the way of the mailbag that he can get for his proposals.

The names and addresses of federal officials you might want to contact are given in appendix 3.

National Consumer Groups

National consumer groups do a good job for the people they try to represent, but you may never know it because they don't have the money or staff to assist consumers directly. The group concentrating on automobiles is the Center for Auto Safety, started in 1967 by Ralph Nader to put pressure on the Department of Transportation to strengthen its safety standards. With a small grant from Consumers Union, the center files and codes consumer letters (now over 20,000), pressures the auto industry to concentrate on safety rather than styling, files briefs on the consumer's behalf at the National Highway Traffic Safety Administration, and participates in the rule-making actions of the Department of Transportation.

The Center for Auto Safety is the only organization

working to balance the pressure exerted by the power-ful auto industry. But it is no match for the might of the Big Three. A startling example of the industry's power in high government places is its victory in the protracted debate over whether the car makers should be obliged to produce by 1973 vehicles that would protect their occupants from serious injuries in a crash at thirty miles per hour.

Many experts say the technology exists to meet such a standard—air bags and dashboard padding are two proposals. The center participated in the public meetings, filed lengthy legal documents, and con-ducted extensive engineering tests in support of such a standard. The engineers of the NHTSA found the standard to be technically feasible and socially desir-able. The head of the agency, Douglas Toms, came out in favor of such a standard and the Secretary of Transportation was privately supporting the thirty-mile test.

When the rule-making process had been substan-tially completed in September 1971 with the recom-mendation of the NHTSA that the standard be en-acted, word came into the secretary's office that the standard would not become effective until the 1976 model year, a substantial victory for the auto indus-try.

Despite the severe setback, the Center for Auto Safety continues to speak loudly for the 100 million car owners in the U.S. It has instigated numerous re-call campaigns and has researched the problems of new-car buyers, particularly their problems with war-ranties. The center is the institution into which Ralph Nader funnels the thousands of letters he receives on car complaints.

Although the center won't be able to solve your complaint individually, or even answer your letter, it should get your mail. It needs such letters for ammunition for its charges that the auto industry should change its way of doing business and for information to be used in tracing patterns of defects in particular automobiles. Besides, just the notation that a copy of your letter is going to Ralph Nader may help you. The center also is interested in hearing what kind of response you did or did not receive from your original complaint letter.

(If you live in Cleveland, Ohio, the Washington, D.C. area, or Hartford, Connecticut, there are local groups affiliated with the Center for Auto Safety which will intervene on your behalf with a safety or repair complaint against local car dealers. They are the Cleveland Auto Safety Research Center, the Maryland Auto Safety Research Center in College Park, and the Connecticut Citizen Action Group in Hartford. See the state-by-state listing of government agencies and consumer groups for the addresses.)

There are a few other national consumer groups which are working hard on your behalf and which also could use your complaint even though they can't help you individually. A relatively new and increasingly influential group is the Washington-based Consumer Federation of America, a coalition of local consumer groups and unions.

One of the oldest and most respected consumer groups is Consumers Union. You might think that forty years ago no one needed a consumer organization. But a handful of scientists, writers, and technicians thought there was a need and that is how Consumers Union and its official magazine *Consumer Reports* were born.

Its development was precarious at first. When it began in 1938 it was faced by an advertising boycott and labeled as a subversive effort undermining the free enterprise system. The organization weathered that stormy period. Today, with a monthly circulation of 2,000,000, an annual budget of $12 million, and a staff of 350, Consumers Union is recognized as the nation's leading consumer organization.

CU was first to do brand name testing by employing trained scientists using sophisticated techniques and then publishing the results. Testers purchase automobiles and other articles for experiments on the open market. The tests are designed to determine the composition and integrity of a product, its safety, and its usefulness. CU also analyzes guarantees and warranties and studies pricing patterns. Every year CU publishes an *Auto Buying Guide,* the authoritative word on the economy, safety, and repair records of new cars.

CU helped Ralph Nader get started by establishing the Ralph Nader Auto Safety Fellowship. CU is still largely responsible for the funding of Nader's Center for Auto Safety.

While CU cannot do much to help you individually, it uses information consumers send in to initiate investigations into dangerous products and other consumer problems. Last year, in response to several letters, CU wrote an article alerting the public to the hazard posed by 1965 through 1969 full-size Fords, some of which were losing their wheels because of a design defect in the lower control arm. CU was largely responsible for the DOT consumer bulletin program whereby a press release announces possible safety hazards without waiting for a full-fledged recall campaign.

To continue to be an effective voice for consumers everywhere, CU needs the continued support of its readers and those in the general public who can alert them to possible hazards in the marketplace.

Legislators in some states are beginning to realize that specialized laws or regulations are needed to deal with consumer problems that can't be properly policed by general criminal-fraud statutes, which are tough to prosecute under and often provide little practical relief for individual consumers.

In one major step, California passed a law which requires every auto repair dealer in the state to register annually with a newly created Bureau of Automotive Repair. The new bureau, which went into business in mid-1972, has jurisdiction over repair work performed, deceptive practices and fraud, and even relationships with customers. The law was hailed by Governor Ronald Reagan as "the toughest and most significant consumer protection legislation of the year in California." Show-biz people sometimes have a way of overstating things. But, in this case, ex-movie actor Reagan may well prove to be right.

Under the California auto repair law, customers must be provided with written estimates and replaced parts upon request. Also, all repair business must post a sign showing the telephone number of the Bureau of Automotive Repair and advising that complaints about service may be referred to the bureau. The law contains provisions for denial, suspension, and revocation of licenses as well as criminal penalties or fines up to $1000 and six months in jail.

Other states are considering new auto repair regulations. In Massachusetts, a Legislative Special Commission on the Motor Vehicle Industry was named to investigate guaranteed auto repairs, licensing of repair shops, registration of mechanics, establishment of a Bureau of Retail Automobile Sales and Automobile Repairs, and creation of an ombudsman board to handle consumer complaints about defective cars and poor repairs.

For now, however, the growing number of city and county agencies have the greatest potential for consumer protection. They are on the scene and have a stake in keeping frauds out of town. A growing number of U.S. cities and counties have specially designated consumer protection offices.

The addresses of the major national consumer groups are given in appendix 3.

State and Local Groups

Your best hope in prodding action or getting intervention on your side may lie with state and local government agencies and consumer groups.

At the state level, attorneys general increasingly are establishing consumer protection offices and use complaints as a basis for legal action. Consumer protection offices are also being created by various state-level agencies to handle complaints that don't involve law violations. Forty-five states, Puerto Rico, and the Virgin Islands now have more than seventy consumer protection offices of one type or another.

The attorney general usually operates under statutory power as the "chief law officer for the state and all departments." The consumer fraud unit processes and investigates complaints and keeps files on businesses according to the frequency with which they are the subject of complaints.

If it is a speedy resolution of your dispute that you need, the criminal process, which cranks along slowly, is not what you want. But the attorney general, in cooperation with local law enforcement authorities, is the only person who can get the fraudulent operators out of the garages and behind bars. His office should get a copy of your letter.

New York City probably has the most active department of consumer affairs. This is largely due to its director, Bess Myerson Grant, who has been able to get funds and publicity for the unit. She has a large staff and launches shotgun investigations without advance notice, thus keeping the business community on its toes. Letters and phone calls are the unit's greatest source of information.

Nassau County in New York has one of the most active county organizations, with enabling legislation which gives the commissioner of the Office of Consumer Affairs wide investigatory powers and duties "to receive and investigate complaints and initiate his own investigations of frauds or unfair dealings against consumers; to hold hearings, compel the attendance of witnesses, administer oaths, take the testimony of any person under oath and in connection therewith require the production of any evidence relating to any matter under investigation or in question before the Commissioner."

Later legislation was enacted which gave to the Office of Consumer Affairs enforcement and injunctive powers through the use of the civil courts of the county. The commissioner may adopt rules and regulations necessary to effectuate the purposes of this new legislation after notice and the holding of a public hearing. The act also gives the commissioner the authority to seek a civil penalty of $500 for each violation and/or injunctive relief. Such actions will be brought by the county attorney upon the request of the commissioner.

Another county consumer protector—the Consumer Protection Division of Dade County, Florida, in Miami—has a specific "Truth in Motor Vehicles Repairs and Estimate Ordinance" in its arsenal. The law requires auto repair dealers to give customers the option of canceling a repair job or authorizing higher charges before going ahead with repairs that will boost the repair bill above the dealer's estimate by $10 or 10 percent, whichever is less.

Of course, if you are cheated you can also take your complaint to local law enforcement agencies. But most police departments are too busy with things like murders and muggings to give more than token attention to consumer grievances. Unfortunately, cheating consumers too often isn't thought of as a crime.

One notable exception is in Houston, Texas, where law and order is being applied to consumerism with great success. There the Consumer Frauds Division of the Harris County sheriff's department acts on legitimate consumer complaints, not by giving a slap on the wrist to offending businesses, but by actually filing criminal charges and making arrests, often with plenty of publicity. The flamboyant head of the division, Sgt. Marvin Zindler, has even been known to take along TV camera crews when making an arrest.

Knowing they face serious charges or bad publicity,

businesses which before ignored consumer complaints now are quick to settle them. In its first three months of operation, the sheriff's Consumer Frauds Division filed over seventy criminal charges and successfully arbitrated more than 1000 more, most in favor of consumers.

Some local consumer protection agencies often will actually intervene and help settle consumer complaints including those on auto repairs. In Maryland's Prince Georges County, outside Washington, D.C., the system works this way in some auto repair disputes: An independent mechanic will go over the car to see what repairs have or have not been made and how well they have been made. Then he submits a report to the Prince Georges County Consumer Council. The disgruntled car owner and the mechanic who wants his bill paid then appear before an arbitration panel which has the independent report. The original mechanic and the car owner then argue their points. The panel decides who gets what.

The Lexington, Kentucky, Citizens Commission for Consumer Protection sponsored establishment of a Lexington-Fayette County Automobile Repair Review Board after determining that "automobiles and automobile repairs generate more complaints than any other consumer item." The review board basically is designed to arbitrate automotive complaints against participating dealers, garages, and service stations.

Local consumer groups also may be able to help you press your complaints. Most such groups have small or volunteer staffs and can't tackle individual complaints. But they can use them to help press for broader reforms or investigations. Some groups, however, will pitch right in and help you lobby for a just settlement of your grievance.

One of the most feisty consumer groups is the Consumer Education and Protective Association of Philadelphia. With seven branches throughout the city, CEPA will try to negotiate a settlement for a victimized consumer first by letter, then by sending a delegation to the company involved. If that doesn't work CEPA goes to bat with picket lines, protest signs, loudspeakers, and similar tactics to press a settlement.

CEPA is a defender especially of the low-income consumer who may be a victim of outright fraud but simply can't afford a lawyer to get his due. The group's militant tactics frequently work wonders, and its victories include many involving auto repair garages and car dealers. CEPA is expanding and has set up offices in at least six more cities—Paterson, New Jersey; Cleveland, Ohio; San Francisco, California; Reno, Nevada; Des Moines, Iowa; and Washington, D.C.

Another active consumer group, the Virginia Citizens Consumer Council, has set up "Good Guy" and "Caution" files on various businesses, including auto repair dealers. The files are based on surveys of Virginia consumers and members of VCCC, which was founded by a group of consumer-minded housewives.

Appendix 3 contains a state-by-state listing of state and local government agencies and local consumer groups that you can contact.

chapter 18 ────────────────

Court Action

If wearing down the garage doesn't work in your case, there still is a way to get your money back for a faulty repair—take the garage to court. Most consumers don't go that far. They figure court action is too complicated and the expense of hiring a lawyer will cost more than the damage.

In many auto repair cases, hiring a lawyer and filing a lawsuit isn't a practical move. But there still is a simple way to get your complaint before a judge, and you don't even need a lawyer: take it to small claims court.

Small Claims Court

Small claims court was created in 1938 to provide an informal, inexpensive tribunal for people who wish to sue for relatively small amounts. Until recently, however, small claims courts have functioned more as a collection agency for large credit merchants and finance companies. This has been changing over the past few years. Through the efforts of Neighborhood Legal Services, junior bar associations, and third-year law students, the court is once again opening to the people.

The procedure in small claims court is so simple that a lawyer is not necessary. In fact, some courts bar attorneys altogether. And in recent years the amount of money that can be recovered has been boosted in some states, reflecting the rise in the cost of living. Maryland recently raised its limit from $2500 to $5000. The amount for which you can sue ranges from a low of only $100 in South Carolina to $5000 in Virginia. But in most states the maximum is under $1000.

The cost of filing a suit in small claims court is low, usually only a few dollars.

To file, you go to the clerk of the small claims court and fill out a short form which asks for the name of the parties, the amount of money in controversy, and a brief description of what took place. You sign the form. The clerk sets a court date, usually within a few weeks. In some courts you can request an evening or Saturday session. Then a summons will go by registered mail or via a court marshal to the party you are suing, notifying him that he must appear in court to answer your charges.

Frequently the suit ends here. The person being sued may take you more seriously, now that you have formalized your charges. An official court summons can do the work of countless telephone calls and letters. In many cases, an otherwise immovable mechanic will offer to pay the amount in dispute.

Another way you will prevail without an actual hearing is if the mechanic does not show up in court. He may decide he doesn't want to lose the time at work or that he doesn't have a chance of convincing the judge. In that case, the judge will usually look at the form you filled out and, unless your story lacks merit on its face, you will win by default; that is, the judge will enter a default judgment against the mechanic, which orders him to pay the money. Unless the mechanic has a very good reason for missing the court date, he will not be allowed to have the default judgment set aside.

When both parties do show up, they go before a judge who will be sitting without a jury. In all but a handful of states, the court procedure is informal and the judge ignores technicalities. In fact, the actual hearing is more like a three-way conversation than a courtroom procedure. You tell your side of the story to the judge and the other party tells his side.

It is important that you have with you any supporting documents such as repair orders, bills, estimates, or car parts. If there were any witnesses, they should be at the hearing. A witness in an auto repair case might be someone who was with you when you took your car for repairs or when you picked it up, or another mechanic who looked over the car for you and can corroborate your story. Often, a written statement from a mechanic is all that is necessary.

After both of you finish telling the judge what happened, he may ask a few questions. Seldom does the whole proceeding take longer than fifteen minutes because of the large number of cases each judge has to hear. He will probably decide immediately and issue an order; or he will decide later and have his clerk notify you.

There is evidence that you are likely to win if you go to court with a legitimate complaint. Consumers Union found that consumers using the small claims courts are getting a fair shake. In 153 cases studied across the country, CU found that 100 of them were settled in favor of the consumer. Ten other cases were settled out of court in the consumer's favor.

Legal Jargon

The last thing you should do is to go into small claims court with the idea you're another Perry Mason. But it's not a bad idea to have some notion of the legal jargon a lawyer might use in a case against a mechanic who gives you a bad shake.

Suppose you took your car to a garage for a mileage check-up, including an oil change. You pick up the car, pay the bill, and drive off. A short time later, the car begins to make a clunking noise. It gets louder, so you pull into a filling station. The attendant finds that you have a broken rod. The reason: although the mechanic charged you for three quarts of oil and a new filter, the same sludge is still in there.

You go back to the garage with your tale of woe. They say it is your fault and share no responsibility.

The first thought that comes to mind is that the mechanic cheated you. He charged you for a new oil filter and an oil change, and he didn't provide either. But try to prove such a charge. Fraud requires proof beyond a reasonable doubt that there was intent to obtain something of value (your money) by a misrepresentation. You may be sure the mechanic did it on purpose, but it is easy for him to argue that it was an honest mistake.

Rather than try to convince the judge the mechanic was out to defraud you, it would be better to say the mechanic agreed to make certain repairs to your car and didn't do them properly. Under the principles of negligence, he would then be liable for the loss you suffered. A lawyer would put it like this: The mechanic holds himself out as a person skilled in automotive service. If he sets out to work on your car, he has a duty to conform to a standard of care that would be exercised by a reasonable man in his profession. His failure to conform—when he did not change the oil and replace the filter—caused damage to your car. The failure to conform is called negligence and he has to pay for your losses.

Neighborhood Legal Services lawyers contend that garages which post signs that read "factory trained mechanic" or "foreign car specialist" should be held to a higher degree of care and skill. This point has not been tested yet in the courts.

You could also argue that the mechanic is guilty of a breach of contract. When you sign the repair order, you and the mechanic enter into a contract. He promises to make certain repairs described on the order, and in return you promise to pay him. If either party fails to keep his side of the bargain, the contract is breached and the other party will get damages for his loss. In the situation just described, the mechanic would pay for an oil change, a new filter, plus the cost of repairs necessitated by his failure to make the repairs properly according to the contract. He would probably have to pay the customer for a new engine.

Take a case where the breach is not so apparent. You take your car to have the carburetor cleaned and pay $30 for the job. The next day, you notice that the car is still stalling and sputtering. You lift off the air cleaner and look into the carburetor and, indeed, it looks soiled with little particles of metal and specks of dirt. You go back to the garage but they contend the work was done.

To take this case to court, you need to allege that there was a contract between you and the mechanic in which he was to clean the carburetor and you were to pay him $30. Although you kept your side of the bargain—payment of the $30—there is compelling evidence that the mechanic did not keep his. You might want to have another mechanic verify that the carburetor is still dirty. Sometimes, just telling this to the judge in court is enough. (Ordinarily this would be hearsay evidence, but it is frequently admitted in small claims court. It would be better, of course, if you could get the mechanic's diagnosis in writing.) In a higher court you would want to bring the second mechanic to court or at least get a written affidavit from him on his findings.

In suing for breach of contract, it isn't necessary that the work not have been done at all. It is enough that the work has been so improperly or unskillfully done that it was of no value or that it was less valuable to you than what you originally bargained for.

The principles of contract are being used more and more in consumer cases in court. The requirements of proof are less stringent and the situations that give rise to dissatisfaction in transactions between mechanics and car owners generally fit into the contract pattern.

Damages, the lawyer's word for your out-of-pocket losses, are totaled up in several ways. One way is to allow the dissatisfied car owner the amount of money it costs to get his car back in working order. Another is the difference between the value of the vehicle in its defective condition and its value in the condition in which it would have been if it had been repaired in compliance with the contract.

These amounts usually work out to be about the same. Asking for other expenses that are ordinarily incurred when your car is out of service, such as cab and bus fare, rental cars, and towing charges, is not a bad idea. Formerly the courts did not recognize these consequential damages, but they are beginning to now. So far, no one has recovered incidental damages, such as a missed business deal.

In summary, the consumer movement hasn't promoted small claims court to a great degree. Some consumer advocates complain that a victory in small claims court is only a Band-Aid over a large wound; the offender pays a piddling amount and goes off again to cheat others. Most consumer groups go for cosmic reform. In the process they overlook the little guy with his $150 repair bill and a car that won't work.

Consumer groups need your support and complaints. But if it is your money you want back, there is little question that small claims court is fast, inexpensive, and more efficient.

Consumer protection agencies in New York, California, Virginia, and Rhode Island, offer free booklets entitled "How to Sue in Small Claims Court."

In New York, write:

City of New York Department of Consumer Affairs
80 Lafayette Street
New York, New York 10013

In California, write:

California Department of Consumer Affairs
1020 N. Street
Sacramento, California 95814

In Virginia, write:

Virginia Department of Agriculture and Commerce
P.O. Box 1163
Richmond, Virginia 23219

In Rhode Island, write:

Rhode Island Consumer Council
365 Broadway
Providence, Rhode Island 02902

Appendix 4 is a guide to small claims courts in the United States, reprinted with the permission of Consumers Union from an article which appeared in its October 1971 issue of *Consumer Reports.*

Lawsuits

Despite the alternative of small claims courts, there may be times when you want to hire a lawyer, especially if the damages to you are extensive or unusually complex. Sometimes, just a letter written on your behalf by an attorney will prod the garage into a more conciliatory stance. If you can't afford a lawyer, check with the local Legal Aid Society for assistance.

The courts are coming down increasingly on the side of aggrieved consumers in consumer fraud cases, so—despite the expenses involved—you may have a good chance of winning your case. A recent New Jersey court ruling in the case of one angry consumer who was oversold and overcharged on repairs at a gas station offers hope to those with complaints against franchised service stations.

Frank Gizzi, a New Jersey motorist, had his brakes repaired at his local Texaco station. The next day, the brakes failed and Mr. Gizzi ran into a tractor trailer. Instead of arguing with his local station, which refused to satisfy his claim, he hired an attorney and sued the Texaco Corporation directly. Mr. Gizzi alleged that Texaco had clothed that station operator with apparent authority to make the necessary repairs, and that he, as a buyer, had reasonably assumed that Texaco would be responsible for any defects.

Further, he introduced evidence showing that Texaco exercised control over its service stations, that the slogan, "Trust your car to the man who wears the star," was permanently displayed at the station and that such slogan was used for purposes of national advertising to convey the impression that Texaco dealers were skilled in automotive service and backed up by the parent corporation.

Mr. Gizzi won. All the major oil companies advertise in a similar manner and all represent that their franchised stations are reputable and responsible businesses. This case sets a precedent for bypassing the station and getting your money back directly from the oil company.

When Patrick Welsh, an Alexandria, Virginia, high school teacher, had his car break down the day after a Gulf station had supposedly fixed it, he had it towed back to the same station. Diagnosis: the starter which the gas station had installed was broken. Instead of replacing the faulty part, however, the station manager told Mr. Welsh, "Take your car and your starter out of here. If we repaired everything that came back in here for free, we'd be out of business."

Mr. Welsh had his car towed to another gas station, where he was informed that the "new" starter installed at the Gulf outlet was actually a used part. The school teacher paid for a new starter. But he then asked a lawyer for help. Gulf Oil Corporation got a letter citing the incident and the Gizzi case. Mr. Welsh got his money back.

Class Action Lawsuits

There is one other type of legal action that offers great potential for aggrieved consumers with monetarily small complaints. This is the class action lawsuit. Its name is derived from the fact that in such suits consumers with similar complaints against a product or company in effect ban together as a "class" and pool their complaints to multiply the damages into a large amount.

In practice, one or more consumers with a small complaint files his suit on behalf of all those with a similar gripe. If they win, the defendant has to pay the total awarded damages to the court. The individual members of the class then can file their own claims and recover damages out of the money held by the court.

The advantage of a class action lawsuit is that it enables a consumer with a small complaint to interest a lawyer in handling his case. Instead of, say, only

$50 damages on a defective car, the lawyer can sue on behalf of thousands of consumers with the same defect for millions of dollars. Since he receives a percentage of the final recovery, he's going to be more willing to press such a case.

The other advantage is that it gives the individual consumer more clout. Tell General Motors you're going to sue them over a defect that costs $50 to fix and they will laugh in your face. But if they know your $50 complaint can quickly multiply to millions of dollars in a class action suit, they will treat your gripe with more respect.

Class action lawsuits, however, still are primarily of only potential benefit to the average consumer. Unclear and narrowly interpreted state laws have rendered class suits impractical in many states. (One notable exception is California, where the state supreme court has upheld the legality of class actions.) Congress so far has bowed to strong business opposition and has failed to pass federal class action legislation.

In addition, class actions aren't likely to be a quick and effective remedy if you just want to get your money back. Such suits are complex affairs that can take years to settle. On the other hand, they are likely to put tremendous pressure on the companies involved to correct legitimate grievances.

In the long run, class action lawsuits may be the lone consumer's greatest weapon in pressing complaints against the giant corporations which increasingly control today's marketplace. It is worth taking the time to write your congressman to urge his support for a federal law allowing you the right to take such legal action.

chapter 19 _____

Delicensing and Criminal Complaints

If you feel you've been defrauded by a repair shop, there are two other steps you can take in an effort to get your money back or to put the offending concern out of business. If the garage is licensed, you can file your complaint with the appropriate licensing board which has the power to take away or suspend the garage's license. Or your complaint to state or local prosecutors could help lead to an investigation and the issuance of a criminal complaint against the garage.

In either case, of course, it usually will take more than just your single grievance to generate either delicensing or a criminal complaint. But if you've really been defrauded, chances are you're not the only victim. Your letter, along with those from others, can help build a case against the garage in question.

Also be aware that neither delicensing nor a criminal complaint is automatically going to get your money back. But such actions, especially a conviction on a criminal complaint, can give you solid ground on which to file your own lawsuit to collect damages. Short of that, just seeking such actions may well make the recalcitrant garage more ready to settle your grievance.

Delicensing

Not all repair garages are licensed. But for those that are, the threat of losing that license can be an imposing one. New-car dealers almost always are licensed, generally by the state motor vehicles department. Many independent garages must get operating permits from local licensing boards. Garages in some states are licensed by the state to perform mandatory auto inspections.

Without such licenses, such garages would be out of business—or, in case of state inspections, out of a substantial amount of business—so they presumably should be sensitive to complaints to licensing agencies about their operations. Unfortunately, this isn't always true, because the licensing agencies often are more interested in raising revenues from issuing the licenses than policing the actions of the license holders.

But the wave of consumerism and the establishment of aggressive consumer protection divisions in the offices of more and more state attorneys general are beginning to change this. The attorney general's office of Wisconsin, for example, has stepped up its efforts to seek suspensions of licenses of car dealers engaging in deceptive practices. In one case it asked the division of motor vehicles to suspend for thirty days the license of a Ford dealer charged with such deceptive tactics as promising prospective used-car buyers free repairs on cars and then requiring the buyer to pay for the repairs.

Car dealers, however, have strong lobbies and the

motor vehicle divisions in Wisconsin and many other states haven't suspended or revoked dealer licenses in years. Because of such traditional inaction, the attorney general's office in Wisconsin is planning, if necessary, to seek other means of policing offending dealers, such as prosecuting them under public nuisance statutes. Such prosecutors would be aided in their delicensing efforts by more complaints from the public.

Meanwhile, some state legislatures are moving to strengthen their licensing procedures and requirements to protect consumers. The state of Maryland now requires each new-car dealer to post a $100,000 bond to back up promises in the new-car warranty.

Few states have gone so far as to license mechanics. While most states have a general license law which authorizes the issuance of specific rules and regulations governing the licensing of persons in various trades and professions, only Connecticut requires that mechanics take a test before they can ply their trade. Senator Hart commented on this situation during his hearings: "The consumer who visits the barber, or beautician, the podiatrist, or plumber knows that to receive their licenses certain skills were necessary. Yet anyone can hold himself out as an expect mechanic, although human lives literally may depend on how well he knows and performs his job."

Several states have mechanic licensing laws pending as a result of the publicity brought to bear on the auto repair industry during Senator Hart's hearings. Many people support licensing laws. But the automobile lobby is a powerful one and, to date, bills have been stymied by the auto industry's concerted efforts to defeat their passage.

Citizen action at the state level could counter the automobile lobby. By writing to your state representative, you can register your support for a program of licensing auto repair facilities and mechanics. Under such a system, you could at least have the assurance that the garage mechanic who, after a cursory inspection of your car's innards, tells you the shocks are shot and the points are pitted, didn't walk in off the street yesterday, pick up a wrench, and call himself a mechanic.

In the meantime, an industry group has announced plans to begin a voluntary program to "certify" mechanics. As of fall 1972, the newly formed National Institute for Automotive Service Excellence offers the nation's estimated 800,000 mechanics opportunities to take a battery of tests to measure their general mechanical competency. Later, tests will be offered in specialties, such as transmission repairs.

Each mechanic who passes the tests will be entitled to display an insignia identifying him as a "Certified General Automobile Mechanic." The institute hopes to test as many as 30,000 mechanics in its first year with each participating mechanic—or his boss—paying a $40 fee.

The testing group was bankrolled by U.S. auto companies, and the National Automobile Dealers Association. Its incorporators include two auto dealers and the past president of the Independent Garage Owners Association. The voluntary program was praised by Senator Hart as a step in the right direction, but he added that he still sees the need to press for federal legislation to require mechanics to be licensed.

It's likely that more than a voluntary effort will be needed to cover the problem. The mechanic who fixes your car should undergo a test at least as stringent as the one you undergo to drive it. An incompetent under the hood is every bit as dangerous as one behind the wheel.

Currently, however, delicensing efforts are pretty much restricted to businesses. In deciding whether to file a complaint with your state licensing board, you must take into consideration the purpose for which licenses are given in your state. There are two general types of state licensing laws applicable to the automobile business—the regulatory business license, with which this chapter will be concerned, and the fiscal or revenue-raising license.

Regulatory business licenses are enacted under the state's inherent police power to protect the public's health, safety, morals, and general welfare and usually provide that detailed requirements must be satisfied before issuance of a license to an applicant. Even more important, the licensing board can revoke the license of an automobile business that does not toe the line. Specific grounds for denial, suspension, or revocation of a license are set forth and an administrative agency or commission is charged with the responsibility of enforcing and implementing the law.

The fiscal registration license, on the other hand, is primarily designed to raise revenue under the state's taxing powers.

The line between these two types of license is not always clear. Take your driver's license, for instance. You must take a test to be licensed to drive. After that first test most drivers just pay a periodic fee to keep the license in effect, usually without being re-tested. So the driver's license is at first regulatory. It later becomes revenue producing.

Some dealer and repairman licensing statutes are like your driver's license. While essentially fiscal in nature, they permit the establishment of rules and regulations which can be used to delicense renegade licensees. The strongest of these spell out specific acts which a dealer or repairman is prohibited from doing if he wishes to do business in the state.

These statutes not only provide for licensing of dealers but also require licenses for manufacturers, their branches, distributors, and agents. In some instances, salesmen must also be licensed. In addition, specific grounds are set forth for the denial, suspension, or revocation of a license, and penalties, including fines and imprisonment, are imposed for violations of the law. Many require the posting of a bond.

Among the grounds on which licenses generally can be revoked or suspended, the following would be of the most interest to car owners: misrepresentation in advertising, defrauding customers, unfair methods of competition, unconscionable business practices, charging excessive interest, and failing to abide by a written agreement.

Here is a typical statement in legal terms of how a license can be suspended or revoked.

LICENSES, HOW DENIED, SUSPENDED OR RE-VOKED. A license may be denied, suspended, or revoked on the following grounds:

1. Proof of unfitness.

2. Material misstatement in application for license.

3. Filing a materially false or fraudulent income tax return as certified by the department of taxation.

4. Willful failure to comply with any provision of this section or any rule or regulation promulgated by the commissioner under this section.

5. Willfully defrauding any retail buyer to the buyer's damage.

6. Willful failure to perform any written agreement with any retail buyer.

7. Failure or refusal to furnish and keep in force any bond required.

8. Having made a fraudulent sale, transaction, or repossession.

9. Fraudulent misrepresentation, circumvention, or concealment through whatsoever subterfuge or device of any of the material particulars or the nature thereof required hereunder to be stated or furnished to the retail buyer.

10. Employment of fraudulent devices, methods, or practices in connection with compliance with the requirements under the statutes of this state with respect to the retaking of goods under retail installment contracts and the redemption and resale of such goods.

11. Having indulged in any unconscionable practice relating to said business.

12. Having charged interest in excess of 15 percent per annum.

13. Having sold a retail installment contract to a sales finance company not licensed hereunder.

14. Having violated any law relating to the sale, distribution, or financing of motor vehicles.

15. Having accepted an order of purchase or a

contract from a buyer, which offer of purchase or contract is subject to subsequent acceptance by the licensee, if such arrangement results in the practice of bushing. For the purpose of this section, bushing is defined as the practice of increasing the selling price of a car above that originally quoted the purchaser after the purchaser has made an initial payment, with either money or trade-in, and signed a purchase order or contract which is subject to subsequent acceptance by the licensee.

16. Having advertised, printed, displayed, published, distributed, broadcast or televised, or caused or permitted to be advertised, printed, displayed, published, distributed, broadcast or televised in any manner whatsoever, any statement or representation with regard to the sale or financing of motor vehicles which is false, deceptive, or misleading.

If you feel that a business you have been dealing with is guilty of any of the listed offenses, you should write to the licensing agency requesting that they review the situation. It is not likely that one letter will induce a licensing board to revoke a license; however, a number of letters should get an investigation under way. A smart businessman will not want to chance losing his operating license; a copy of a letter to the state licensing board sent to your garage may be worth countless angry phone calls and visits to a recalcitrant repairman.

The following states have strong licensing statutes; if you live in one, write these agencies with your complaint:

Arkansas—Department of Motor Vehicles
Arizona—Motor Vehicle Department

Colorado—Motor Vehicle Dealer's Administrator; Director of Revenue

Connecticut—Commissioner of Motor Vehicles

Delaware—Motor Vehicle Department

Florida—Director of Department of Motor Vehicles

Georgia—State Board of Registration of Used Car Dealers (composed of used car dealers)

Hawaii—Motor Vehicle Licensing Board

Idaho—Department of Law Enforcement

Illinois—Secretary of State

Kansas—Department of Motor Vehicles

Kentucky—Department of Motor Transportation

Louisiana—Motor Vehicle Commission (composed of dealers)

Maryland—Department of Motor Vehicles (now requires dealer to post $100,000 bond to back up promises in warranty)

Massachusetts—Police Commissioner in Boston (and licensing authorities in other cities)

Mississippi—Motor Vehicle Commission

Montana—Registrar of Motor Vehicles

Nebraska—Motor Vehicle Dealers License Board; Director of Motor Vehicles and Dealers

Nevada—Department of Motor Vehicles

New Jersey—Director of Motor Vehicles

New Mexico—Division of Motor Vehicles

North Carolina—Department of Motor Vehicles

North Dakota—Registrar of Motor Vehicles

Oklahoma—Motor Vehicle Commission (composed of dealers)

Oregon—Department of Motor Vehicles

Pennsylvania—Secretary of Revenue; State Board of Motor Vehicle Salesmen

Rhode Island—Motor Vehicle Dealers License Commission (composed of dealers)

South Carolina—State Highway Department

Tennessee—Motor Vehicle Commission (composed of dealers)

Texas—Highway Department

Utah—Motor Vehicle Dealer's Administrator (with advisory board of licensed dealers)

Virginia—Commissioner of the Division of Motor Vehicles

Washington—Director of Licenses

West Virginia—Department of Motor Vehicles

Wisconsin—Motor Vehicle Department

The Criminal Complaint

The main criminal law tools available to protect the consumer reach only the most flagrant types of consumer fraud and deceptions. Even when they are applicable, local officials often are not able to enforce these statutes because their time is taken up by more violent crimes.

In some situations, the state and county prosecutors have the criminal law available to help protect the public against fraudulent operators. Consumer abuses usually fall under the false pretense statute or the false advertising statute.

Proving false pretenses is difficult. The plaintiff must show intent and prove that the garageman's fraud related not to what he said he would do but to what he did. Thus, the mechanic who promises to put your car in good working order is not guilty of false pretenses when you drive 500 feet out of the garage and your engine blows a rod because he failed to put the oil plug back in. This is because his statement referred to what he was going to do, not to what he has already done—so, not guilty. But the mechanic who writes up a bill listing repairs he knows were not made could be found guilty of false pretenses.

The false advertising statutes, where they exist, frequently fail because the broadcasters and publishers through whom most of the bait-and-switch advertising is funneled are not prosecuted. Much advertising is ambiguous and hard to label deceptive and, as everyone who watches television knows, "puffing" is allowed.

The criminal law is not an appropriate tool to achieve broad social policy changes. There is general consensus that the criminal law in many states is inadequate to achieve comprehensive consumer protection. A criminal complaint requires almost the impossible—proof of a state of mind, beyond a reasonable doubt. And, if a prosecution is won, many times the penalties and fines imposed are light and chalked up by the offenders as the cost of doing business.

Couple this with the widespread reluctance of local officials to prosecute seemingly respectable businessmen and you have a consumer getting little protection from his law enforcement officials in the marketplace.

Still, it is worth your time to write or call the responsible law enforcement officials in your state, county, and city. Some states are beefing up their consumer fraud units in response to pressure from irate citizens. The attorney generals' offices in California, New York, and Washington, D.C., report that convictions against fraudulent auto repairmen have resulted from investigations launched after receipt of complaints from consumers.

In the District of Columbia the U.S. attorney's office prosecuted a hard-core transmission con artist who had operated for several years in Washington and Maryland under various names. The investigation was undertaken in response to several complaints to the U.S. attorney that Riley Ferrebee had charged outrageous prices for transmission repairs that had never been made. The attorney was able to subpoena records and get in touch with Ferrebee's other customers.

The investigation uncovered patterns of misleading advertising, bait-and-switch tactics, and overcharging for repairs that were done, as well as charging for repairs that were never made. Nine victims were named in the suit that was filed. Ferrebee entered a plea of guilty to mail fraud and was sentenced. He has appealed his conviction.

Two Maryland mechanics were sentenced to six-year and ten-year terms respectively in 1971 for auto repair fraud. Calling the pair "thieves," a Maryland court of special appeals judge upheld the convictions of the owner and manager of the Vanguard Auto Service Center in Bethesda.

The top mechanic at Vanguard actually was a steam cleaner who could make used parts look like new. Vanguard mechanics could make old carburetors shine with a super cleaner called "2 Plus 2." Parts that couldn't be cleaned were painted over. In each case, the customer was charged for new parts that were never installed.

The case also provided an example of how you can

take advantage of such court actions to get your money back. After hearing of the criminal convictions of the Vanguard duo, Mrs. Lilous Miller brought a civil action against Vanguard, charging that the shop took $300 from her for repairing an automatic transmission that had never been touched. She settled out of court for approximately $100.

The California attorney general's office actively investigates auto repair practices there and seeks injunctions to stop abuses. It has also adopted techniques in some cases designed to help the victims of such repairs recoup their losses. In one case, for example, the prosecuted company paid a civil penalty of $4000 and agreed to place an additional $3000 in trust in small claims court for the benefit of customers bringing actions against the concern.

Frequently, however, you may just have to settle for the satisfaction of seeing an auto repair con man behind bars and out of business.

One advantage of the criminal complaint is that it requires no lawyer. Your local prosecutor will file the charges for you. In most states a person filing a criminal complaint on auto repair must allege the following:

—Falsity as to past or present fact (the mechanic knows he did not perform repairs charged for)
—Intent (he meant to do what he did)
—You relied on his false representations (by driving car away or by paying bill)
—The mechanic got something of value (your money)
—The mechanic knows what he said was false.

Appendix 1: Estimated Cost of Operating a Car

Estimated Cost of Operating a Standard Size 1972 Model Automobile

(Total costs in dollars, costs per mile in cents)

Item	First Year (14,500 miles) Total Cost	Cost Per Mile	Second Year (13,000 miles) Total Cost	Cost Per Mile	Third Year (11,500 miles) Total Cost	Cost Per Mile	Fourth Year (10,000 miles) Total Cost	Cost Per Mile	Fifth Year (9,900 miles) Total Cost	Cost Per Mile
Costs Excluding Taxes:										
Depreciation	1,226.00	8.46	900.00	6.92	675.00	5.87	500.00	5.00	376.00	3.80
Repairs and Maintenance	81.84	.56	115.37	.89	242.65	2.11	296.09	2.96	275.54	2.78
Replacement Tires	17.90	.12	16.05	.12	23.72	.21	44.40	.44	43.95	.44
Accessories	3.21	.02	3.08	.02	2.96	.02	2.83	.03	2.82	.03
Gasoline	286.75	1.98	257.16	1.98	227.58	1.98	197.72	1.98	195.83	1.98
Oil	11.25	.08	11.25	.09	12.00	.10	12.00	.12	12.75	.13
Insurance[a]	164.00	1.13	156.00	1.20	156.00	1.36	147.00	1.47	147.00	1.49
Garaging, Parking, Tolls, etc.	208.36	1.44	199.22	1.53	190.08	1.65	180.94	1.81	180.33	1.82
Total	1,999.31	13.79	1,658.12	12.75	1,529.99	13.30	1,380.98	13.81	1,234.22	12.47
Taxes and Fees:										
State:										
Gasoline	74.62	.51	66.92	.52	59.22	.52	51.45	.51	50.96	.52
Registration	30.00	.21	30.00	.23	30.00	.26	30.00	.30	30.00	.30
Titling	177.15	1.22	—	—	—	—	—	—	—	—
Subtotal	281.77	1.94	96.92	.75	89.22	.78	81.45	.81	80.96	.82
Federal:										
Gasoline	42.64	.30	38.24	.30	33.84	.29	29.40	.30	29.12	.30
Oil[b]	.22	—	.22	—	.24	—	.24	—	.26	—
Tires	1.38	.01	1.24	.01	1.82	.02	3.42	.03	3.39	.03
Subtotal	44.24	.31	39.70	.31	35.90	.31	33.06	.33	32.77	.33
Total Taxes	326.01	2.25	136.62	1.06	125.12	1.09	114.51	1.14	113.73	1.15
Total of All Costs	2,325.32	16.04	1,794.75	13.81	1,655.11	14.39	1,495.49	14.95	1,347.95	13.62

ITEM	Sixth Year (9,900 miles)		Seventh Year (9,500 miles)		Eighth Year (8,500 miles)		Ninth Year (7,500 miles)		Tenth Year (5,700 miles)		Totals and Averages for Ten Years (100,000 miles)	
	Total Cost	Cost Per Mile	Total Cost	Cost Per Mile	Total Cost	Cost Per Mile	Total Cost	Cost Per Mile	Total Cost	Cost Per Mile	Total Cost	Cost Per Mile
Costs Excluding Taxes:												
Depreciation	259.00	2.61	189.00	1.99	121.00	1.42	85.00	1.13	48.00	.84	4,379.00	4.38
Repairs and Maintenance	292.54	2.95	397.56	4.19	171.82	2.02	244.33	3.26	29.17	.51	2,146.91	2.14
Replacement Tires	45.44	.46	50.69	.53	62.79	.74	52.80	.70	42.11	.74	399.85	.40
Accessories	8.57	.09	8.30	.09	7.65	.09	6.97	.09	5.79	.10	52.18	.05
Gasoline	195.83	1.98	188.03	1.98	168.13	1.98	148.22	1.98	112.71	1.98	1,977.96	1.98
Oil	13.50	.14	13.50	.14	13.50	.16	12.00	.16	6.75	.12	118.50	.12
Insurance(a)	116.00	1.17	116.00	1.22	116.00	1.37	116.00	1.55	116.00	2.04	1,350.00	1.35
Garaging, Parking, Tolls, etc.	180.33	1.82	177.89	1.87	171.80	2.02	165.71	2.21	154.74	2.71	1,809.40	1.81
Total	1,111.21	11.22	1,140.97	12.01	832.69	9.80	831.03	11.08	515.27	9.04	12,233.80	12.23
Taxes and Fees:												
State:												
Gasoline	50.96	.51	48.93	.51	43.75	.52	38.57	.52	29.33	.51	514.71	.51
Registration	30.00	.30	30.00	.32	30.00	.35	30.00	.40	30.00	.53	300.00	.30
Titling	—	—	—	—	—	—	—	—	—	—	177.15	.18
Subtotal	80.96	.82	78.93	.83	73.75	.87	68.57	.92	59.33	1.04	991.86	.99
Federal:												
Gasoline	29.12	.29	27.96	.30	25.00	.29	22.04	.29	16.76	.29	294.12	.30
Oil(b)	.27	—	.27	—	.27	—	.24	—	.14	—	2.37	—
Tires	3.50	.04	3.90	.04	4.84	.06	4.07	.06	3.24	.06	30.80	.03
Subtotal	32.89	.33	32.13	.34	30.11	.35	26.35	.35	20.14	.35	327.29	.33
Total Taxes	113.85	1.15	111.06	1.17	103.86	1.22	94.92	1.27	79.47	1.39	1,319.15	1.32
Total of All Costs	1,225.06	12.37	1,252.03	13.18	936.55	11.02	925.95	12.35	594.74	10.43	13,552.95	13.55

SOURCE: U.S. Office of Highway Planning, Highway Statistics Division

NOTE: This estimate covers the total costs of a fully equipped, medium priced, standard size, 4-door sedan, purchased for $4,379, operated 100,000 miles over a 10-year period, then scrapped. Baltimore area prices, considered to be in the middle range, were used.

a) Previous editions of this study used insurance rates designated for Baltimore city. The rates shown above are for the Baltimore suburbs, and consequently are less than the rates presented in the previous study. If the Baltimore city rates had been used in this study, the insurance costs would have been higher. (For example, the first year would have been $232.)

b) Where costs per mile were computed to be less than 1/20 cent, a dash (—) appears in the column.

217

Estimated Cost of Operating a Compact Size 1972 Model Automobile
(Total costs in dollars, costs per mile in cents)

ITEM	First Year (14,500 miles) Total Cost	Cost Per Mile	Second Year (13,000 miles) Total Cost	Cost Per Mile	Third Year (11,500 miles) Total Cost	Cost Per Mile	Fourth Year (10,000 miles) Total Cost	Cost Per Mile	Fifth Year (9,900 miles) Total Cost	Cost Per Mile
Costs Excluding Taxes:										
Depreciation	674.00	4.65	519.00	3.99	394.00	3.42	305.00	3.05	243.00	2.46
Repairs and Maintenance	79.41	.55	107.14	.83	170.61	1.48	218.90	2.19	240.27	2.43
Replacement Tires	15.30	.11	13.71	.11	12.13	.11	34.27	.34	33.93	.34
Accessories	3.21	.02	3.08	.02	2.96	.03	2.83	.03	2.82	.03
Gasoline	244.25	1.68	218.97	1.69	193.68	1.69	168.39	1.68	166.78	1.68
Oil	10.50	.07	10.50	.08	11.25	.10	11.25	.11	12.75	.13
Insurance	155.00	1.07	147.00	1.13	147.00	1.28	140.00	1.40	140.00	1.41
Garaging, Parking, Tolls, etc.	208.36	1.44	199.22	1.53	190.08	1.65	180.94	1.81	180.33	1.82
Total	1,390.03	9.59	1,218.62	9.38	1,121.71	9.76	1,061.58	10.61	1,019.88	10.30
Taxes and Fees:										
State:										
Gasoline	63.56	.44	56.98	.44	50.40	.44	43.82	.44	43.40	.44
Registration	20.00	.14	20.00	.15	20.00	.17	20.00	.20	20.00	.20
Titling	109.86	.75	—	—	—	—	—	—	—	—
Subtotal	193.42	1.33	76.98	.59	70.40	.61	63.82	.64	63.40	.64
Federal:										
Gasoline	36.32	.25	32.56	.25	28.80	.25	25.04	.25	24.80	.25
Oil[a]	.21	—	.21	—	.22	—	.22	—	.26	—
Tires	1.17	.01	1.05	.01	.92	.01	2.61	.03	2.59	.03
Subtotal	37.70	.26	33.82	.26	29.94	.26	27.87	.28	27.65	.28
Total Taxes	231.12	1.59	110.80	.85	100.34	.87	91.69	.92	91.05	.92
Total of All Costs	1,621.15	11.18	1,329.42	10.23	1,222.05	10.63	1,153.27	11.53	1,110.93	11.22

Item	Sixth Year (9,900 miles)		Seventh Year (9,500 miles)		Eighth Year (8,500 miles)		Ninth Year (7,500 miles)		Tenth Year (5,700 miles)		Totals and Averages for Ten Years (100,000 miles)	
	Total Cost	Cost Per Mile	Total Cost	Cost Per Mile	Total Cost	Cost Per Mile	Total Cost	Cost Per Mile	Total Cost	Cost Per Mile	Total Cost	Cost Per Mile
Costs Excluding Taxes:												
Depreciation	194.00	1.96	152.00	1.60	103.00	1.21	73.00	.97	39.00	.68	2,696.00	2.70
Repairs and Maintenance	268.81	2.72	412.04	4.34	177.27	2.09	78.95	1.05	31.10	.55	1,784.50	1.79
Replacement Tires	38.45	.39	36.89	.39	61.53	.72	54.29	.73	41.27	.72	341.77	.34
Accessories	8.57	.09	8.30	.09	7.65	.09	6.97	.09	5.79	.10	52.18	.05
Gasoline	166.78	1.68	160.06	1.69	143.11	1.69	126.43	1.69	96.03	1.68	1,684.48	1.68
Oil	12.75	.13	12.75	.13	12.75	.15	12.00	.16	6.75	.12	113.25	.11
Insurance	114.00	1.15	114.00	1.20	114.00	1.34	114.00	1.52	114.00	2.00	1,299.00	1.30
Garaging, Parking, Tolls, etc.	180.33	1.82	177.89	1.87	171.80	2.02	165.71	2.21	154.74	2.72	1,809.40	1.81
Total	983.69	9.94	1,073.93	11.31	791.11	9.31	631.35	8.42	488.68	8.57	9,780.58	9.78
Taxes and Fees:												
State:												
Gasoline	43.40	.44	41.65	.44	37.24	.44	32.90	.44	24.99	.44	438.34	.44
Registration	20.00	.20	20.00	.21	20.00	.23	20.00	.26	20.00	.35	200.00	.20
Titling	—	—	—	—	—	—	—	—	—	—	109.86	.11
Subtotal	63.40	.64	61.65	.65	57.24	.67	52.90	.70	44.99	.79	748.20	.75
Federal:												
Gasoline	24.80	.25	23.80	.25	21.28	.25	18.80	.25	14.28	.25	250.48	.25
Oil[a]	.26	—	.26	—	.26	—	.24	—	.13	—	2.27	—
Tires	2.93	.03	2.81	.03	4.69	.06	4.15	.06	3.15	.06	26.07	.03
Subtotal	27.99	.28	26.87	.28	26.23	.31	23.19	.31	17.56	.31	278.82	.28
Total Taxes	91.39	.92	88.52	.93	83.47	.98	76.09	1.01	62.55	1.10	1,027.02	1.03
Total of All Costs	1,075.08	10.86	1,162.45	12.24	874.58	10.29	707.44	9.43	551.23	9.67	10,807.60	10.81

219

SOURCE: U.S. Office of Highway Planning, Highway Statistics Division
NOTE: This estimate covers the total costs of a medium priced, compact size, 2-door sedan, purchased for $2,696, operated 100,000 miles over a 10-year period, then scrapped. Baltimore area prices, considered to be in the middle range, were used.
a) Where costs per mile were computed to be less than 1/20 cent, a dash (—) appears in the column.

Estimated Cost of Operating a Subcompact Size 1972 Model Automobile
(Total costs in dollars, costs per mile in cents)

ITEM	FIRST YEAR (14,500 miles)		SECOND YEAR (13,000 miles)		TOTALS AND AVERAGES FOR TEN YEARS (100,000 miles)	
	Total Cost	Cost Per Mile	Total Cost	Cost Per Mile	Total Cost	Cost Per Mile
Costs Excluding Taxes:						
Depreciation	310.00	2.14	285.00	2.19	2,064.00	2.07
Repairs and Maintenance	76.15	.53	114.59	.88	1,775.71	1.78
Replacement Tires	13.98	.10	12.53	.10	312.29	.31
Accessories	3.21	.02	3.08	.02	52.18	.05
Gasoline	181.84	1.25	163.02	1.25	1,255.15	1.25
Oil	10.50	.07	9.75	.08	103.50	.10
Insurance	145.00	1.00	140.00	1.08	1,251.00	1.25
Garaging, Parking, Tolls, etc.	208.36	1.44	199.22	1.53	1,809.40	1.81
Total	949.04	6.55	927.19	7.13	8,623.23	8.62

220

Taxes and Fees:

	First Year		Second Year		Ten-Year Total	
State:						
Gasoline	47.32	.33	42.42	.33	326.62	.33
Registration	20.00	.14	20.00	.15	200.00	.20
Titling	84.57	.58	—	—	84.57	.08
Subtotal	151.89	1.05	62.42	.48	611.19	.61
Federal:						
Gasoline	27.04	.18	24.24	.19	186.64	.19
Oil[a]	.21	—	.19	—	2.07	—
Tires	.94	.01	.84	.01	20.90	.02
Subtotal	28.19	.19	25.27	.20	209.61	.21
Total Taxes	180.08	1.24	87.69	.68	820.80	.82
Total of All Costs	1,129.12	7.79	1,014.88	7.81	9,444.03	9.44

SOURCE: U.S. Office of Highway Planning, Highway Statistics Division

NOTE: This estimate covers the total costs of a low priced, subcompact size, 2-door sedan, purchased for $2,064, operated 100,000 miles over a 10-year period, then scrapped. Baltimore area prices, considered to be in the middle range, were used. Since cost data for American-made subcompacts does not exist past the second year, only the first, second, and estimated ten-year totals are shown.

a) Where costs per mile were computed to be less than 1/20 cent, a dash (—) appears in the column.

Appendix 2: Major Recall Campaigns

Major Recall Campaigns (over 50,000) of the Largest Domestic and Foreign Car Manufacturers
Period covered: January 1, 1971 to June 30, 1972

DOMESTIC

ADMIN. IDENTI- FICATION NUMBER	DATE OF COM- PANY NOTIFI- CATION	MAKE	MODEL	MODEL YEAR	BRIEF DESCRIPTION OF DEFECT (MANUFACTURER'S CORRECTIVE ACTION)	NO. OF PAGES ON FILE	NUMBER OF VEHICLES RECALLED
					Chrysler Motors Corporation		
71–0070	4–20–71	Plymouth Dodge	Barracuda Challenger	1970 1970	Folding front seat back fitted with self-locking latch which holds back of seat in upright position may not meet requirements of Federal Motor Vehicle Safety Standard No. 207. Purpose of latch is to minimize possibility of injury in event of collision. (Correct by making necessary adjustments.)	6	127,087

71-0173	9-29-71	Chrysler	Chrysler Imperial	1972	Possibility that shaft bushing in transmission control linkage may be inadequately torqued. Loss of bushing from transmission-mounted bracket will create excessive free play in linkage, which could allow operator to shift control lever without having transmission accomplish proper action. (Correct by inspecting and retorquing shaft bushing where necessary.)	15	52,729
		Dodge	Imperial Demon Coronet Charger Polara Monaco	1972			
		Plymouth	Duster Satellite Fury	1972			
72-0145	5-30-72	Plymouth	Fury	1972	Possibility that front bumper guard may not be adequately attached to bumper to withstand loads imposed during jacking. If condition exists, guard could pull off during jacking. (Correct by inspecting and replacing with new bumper jack hook.)	2	56,371

223

SOURCE: U.S. Department of Transportation, *Motor Vehicle Safety Defect Recall Campaigns, 1971, 1972* (Washington, D.C.: Government Printing Office).

Major Recall Campaigns (continued)

ADMIN. IDENTI-FICATION NUMBER	DATE OF COM-PANY NOTIFI-CATION	MAKE	MODEL	MODEL YEAR	BRIEF DESCRIPTION OF DEFECT (MANUFACTURER'S CORRECTIVE ACTION)	NO. OF PAGES ON FILE	NUMBER OF VEHICLES RECALLED
					Ford Motor Company		
71-0045	4-2-71	Ford	Pinto	1971	Possibility that engine backfire may ignite accumulated fuel vapors in air cleaner assembly, creating possibility of fire damage in engine compartment. (Correct by modifying.)	86	215,823
72-0095	4-24-72	Ford	Torino Ranchero	1972	Possibility that rear axle bearing may deteriorate due to high axle shaft deflection. Deterioration of bearing usually will produce sufficient noise and vibration to indicate need for repair; relative movement of axle shaft will result in complete loss of tractive effect as it disengages from differential. (Correct by inspecting and replacing with larger diameter shaft axle and new bearing.)	41	407,244
		Mercury	Montego	1972			

224

| 72-0160 | 6-28-72 | All | Passenger cars (except 1970 Maverick & 1970–1971 convertibles & imports) Ranchero | 1970 1971 | Possibility that shoulder belt pin connector plastic sleeves which were injection molded contains surface imperfection or discontinuity at point at which thermal plastic is injected into mold and where flow diverges to fill both sides of ring. If condition exists and sleeve breaks away from pin, shoulder belt probably will not remain engaged to seat belt buckle, thereby preventing effective use of shoulder harness. (Correct by replacing shoulder belt pin connector plastic sleeve with neoprene retainers.) | 2 | 4,072,000 |
| 72-0161 | 6-28-72 | Ford | Station wagon | 1972 | Possibility that vehicles were assembled with upper portion of rear bumper jacking slot obstructed by rear bumper reinforcement. Condition could prevent engagement of jack hook or could permit partial engagement causing vehicle to possibly disengage from jack while in raised position. (Correct by inspecting and removing obstruction material where necessary.) | 2 | 157,623 |

Major Recall Campaigns (continued)

Admin. Identi-fication Number	Date of Company Notifi- cation	Make	Model	Model Year	Brief Description of Defect (Manufacturer's Corrective Action)	No. of Pages on File	Number of Vehicles Recalled
			General Motors Corporation				
71-0027	2-19-71	GMC	EG, EM, SG, and SM models with mechanical clutch linkage medium duty trucks and school bus chassis	1967 1968 1969	Possibility that clutch idler lever assembly and ball studs located between left frame rail and engine may be subject to breakage. Failure of either idler lever assembly or ball stud will result in positive connection between clutch pedal and clutch assembly causing clutch to be engaged at all times. (Correct by modifying where necessary.)	10	53,700
71-0139	8-18-71	Chevrolet	Blazer K-10, K-20	1969 1970 1971	Possibility that under certain operating conditions front spring may break near front attachment on steering column side. Breakage could cause vehicle to veer toward left in left-hand drive vehicles and to right in right-hand drive vehi-	19	124,000
		GMC	Jimmy's K1500 K2500 All 4-wheel drive				

226

71-0140	8-18-71	Chevrolet	K-20, C-20 C-30.	1971	cles. (Correct by replacing longer second leaf where necessary.) Possibility that power brake vacuum cylinder (booster can) and/or attaching brackets may develop fatigue cracks. If bracket cracks, could permit excessive movement of brake cylinder assembly. Continued operation could crack front hydraulic brake line with resultant loss of brake fluid in part of dual braking system. (Correct by replacing components where necessary.)	14	136,000
		GMC	C2500, K2500 and C3500 (except RPO H-22 w/ 11,000# axle)				
71-0224	11-22-71	Chevrolet	Corvair Corvan	1961 thru 1969	Possibility that fumes in direct air heating system may be transferred from engine compartment into passenger compartment. Such fumes, in some cases, contain carbon monoxide in sufficient concentration to harm or endanger occupants of vehicle. (Correct by inspecting and repairing where necessary.)	11	679,900

227

Major Recall Campaigns (continued)

General Motors Corporation (continued)

Admin. Identi- fication Number	Date of Com- pany Notifi- cation	Make	Model	Model Year	Brief Description of Defect (Manufacturer's Corrective Action)	No. of Pages on File	Number of Vehicles Recalled
71-0235	12-10-71	Chevrolet GMC	Chevrolet Chevy II Nova Camaro Chevrolet Trucks C, P, G GMC Trucks C, P, G	1965 thru 1969 Trucks 1965 thru 1970	Possibility that separated motor mount may allow motor to lift, which may affect throttle linkage, momentarily increasing throttle opening, possibly to full throttle. (Correct by inspecting and installing restraints which will limit engine lift and eliminate possible secondary effects of engine mount separation.)	8	6,682,084
72-0075	4-5-72	Chevrolet	Vega	1972	Possibility that vehicles equipped with engines option L-11 (2 barrel carburetor) may experience exhaust system backfires of sufficient	19	129,000

228

| 72-0112 | 5-5-72 | Chevrolet Vega | 1971 1972 | frequency and magnitude to weaken and rupture muffler. Exhausts from muffler with ruptured end cover can subject fuel tank to sufficient heat to expand fuel and create fuel spillage. Subsequent engine backfires may ignite fuel and cause fire damage. (Correct by inspecting and installing new muffler and components where necessary.) | | |
| | | | | Possibility that vehicles equipped with standard engine and monojet (single barrel) carburetor may experience breakage of idle stop solenoid bracket. Should bracket break, there is possibility that idle solenoid and clamp portion of bracket may drop and lodge in area that can cause throttle to be held in partially open position. (Correct by installing additional new bracket.) | 13 | 350,000 |

Major Recall Campaigns (continued)

ADMIN. IDENTI- FICATION NUMBER	DATE OF COM- PANY NOTIFI- CATION	MAKE	MODEL	MODEL YEAR	BRIEF DESCRIPTION OF DEFECT (MANUFACTURER'S CORRECTIVE ACTION)	NO. OF PAGES ON FILE	NUMBER OF VEHICLES RECALLED
			General Motors Corporation, Buick Division, Opel				
71-0176	10-1-71	Opel	Kadetts Model 31, 31D, 36, 36D and 39-1900 Series	1970 1971 1972	Possibility that windshield may not have been mounted to conform with retention requirement of Federal Motor Vehicle Safety Standard No. 212. If condition exists and vehicle is involved in high impact frontal collision, windshield may come out. (Correct by inspecting and securing with improved adhesive where necessary.)	12	100,561
			Nissan Motor Corporation in U.S.A.				
72-0052	2-29-72	Datsun	LB110 Sedan KL110 Coupe	1971	Possibility of misalignment of secondary hood latch between hood and body, which could result in complete disengagement of hood	2	86,429

230

| 72-0065 | 3-28-72 | Datsun | PL510 Sedan WPL510 Station Wagon | Manfd Aug. 9 1971 thru March 15, 1972 | latch, if primary hood latch has not been properly engaged and if vehicle is subject to strong wind pressure at high speeds. (Correct by inspecting and adjusting position of hood latch.) Possibility that under extreme cold weather and severe driving conditions, front brake hose, which is clamped to shock strut in a manner restricting its free movement, can crack at clamp, due to repeated bending of hose. Should crack occur, could result in loss of brake fluid, and loss of front brake function. (Correct by inspecting and installing spring-hanger type brake hoses.) | 1 | 61,434 |
| 72-0159 | 6-26-72 | Datsun | L520 & L521 | Manfd 4-65 thru 5-69 | Possibility that accelerator pedal pad could lock under travel stop bolt head. If condition exists, depressed accelerator pedal would not return to closed position when released. (Correct by inspecting and installing bolt with larger head to preclude pedal pad from locking up.) | 1 | 62,000 |

Major Recall Campaigns (continued)

Admin. Identi-fication Number	Date of Com-pany Notifi-cation	Make	Model	Model Year	Brief Description of Defect (Manufacturer's Corrective Action)	No. of Pages on File	Number of Vehicles Recalled
			Toyota Motor Sales, U.S.A., Inc.				
71–0084	5–17–71	Toyota	Corona	1965 thru 1970	Possibility that items placed in package tray under the right dash panel may inadvertently fall over protective partition and cause possible malfunction of accelerator linkage. (Correct by installing new partition.)	11	190,000
			Corolla	1970 1971			
72–0014	1–12–72	Toyota	Corolla–1200 Sedan Coupe Station Wagon Corolla 1600 Sedan Coupe Station Wagon	1971 1971	Possibility that engine stall or engine hesitation may occur due to malfunctions in evaporative emission control system. Engine hesitation or stall may be hazardous in road driving due to lack of fuel or loss of power after prolonged high speed driving. (Correct by inspecting and modifying emission control system.)	13	110,614

232

Volkswagen of America, Incorporated

71-0005	12-28-70 Volks-wagen	Type 1, 3, 4, and Super Beetle	1971	Possibility that guide pin in steering column lock may have been damaged in assembly. Also, ignition switch may have manufacturing defect. These conditions could result in difficulty in unlocking steering and starting engine. (Correct by replacing locks and switches where necessary.) Possibility that left front hood hinge may rub against wiring harness causing damage to wiring. (Correct by re-routing wiring harness where necessary.)	21	78,100

Appendix 3: Places to Write To with Your Complaint

Private Companies and Organizations

AUTO MANUFACTURERS

H. G. Nakamura, Vice President
American Honda Motor Co.
100 West Alondra Boulevard
Gardena, California 90247

Roy D. Chapin, Jr., Chairman
American Motors Corp.
14250 Plymouth Road
Detroit, Michigan 48232

Lynn Townsend, Chairman
Chrysler Corp.
341 Massachusetts Avenue
Detroit, Michigan 48231

Byron J. Nichols
Vice President of Consumer Affairs
Chrysler Corp.
(Plymouth, Dodge, Chrysler, Imperial, Colt, Cricket)
P.O. Box 1086
Detroit, Michigan 48231

Vincent Garibaldi, President
Fiat Motor Co., Inc.

375 Park Avenue
New York, New York 10022

Henry Ford II, Chairman
Ford Motor Co.
The American Road
Dearborn, Michigan 48121

Ford Motor Co. Listens
(Ford, Lincoln, Mercury, Capri)
P.O. Box 1958
The American Road #5
Dearborn, Michigan 48121

R. C. Gerstenberg, Chairman
General Motors Corp.
3044 West Grand Boulevard
Detroit, Michigan 48202

GM Divisions:

F. James McDonald, General Manager
Chevrolet Division
3044 West Grand Boulevard
Detroit, Michigan 48202

Martin Caserio, General Manager
Pontiac Division
One Pontiac Plaza
Pontiac, Michigan 48055

John Belt, General Manager
Oldsmobile Division
Townsend Street
Lansing, Michigan 48921

Lee Mays, General Manager
Buick Division
(Opel)
Hamilton Avenue
Flint, Michigan 48550

George Elges, General Manager
Cadillac Division

236

2860 Clark Avenue
Detroit, Michigan 48232

G. W. Whitehead, President
British Leyland Motors Inc.
(Austin, MG, Triumph, Jaguar, Rover)
600 Willow Tree Road
Leonia, New Jersey 07605

Karlfield Nordman, President
Mercedes-Benz of North America
158 Linwood Plaza
Fort Lee, New Jersey 07024

Mazda Motors of America
3040 East Ana Street
Compton, California 90221

Y. Katayama, President
Nissan Motor Corp., U.S.A.
(Datsun)
18501 South Figueroa Street
Gardena, California 90247

Jean Ordner, President
Renault Inc.
100 Sylvan Avenue
Englewood Cliffs, New Jersey 07632

Rolls Royce Inc.
75 Century Road
Box 189
Paramus, New Jersey 07652

Ralph T. Miller, President
Saab-Scania of America, Inc.
Saab Drive
Orange, Connecticut 06477

Subaru of America, Inc.
7040 Central Highway
Pennsauken, New Jersey 08109

Shoji Hattori, President
Toyota Motor Sales, U.S.A.
2055 West 190th Street
Torrance, California 90509

J. Stuart Perkins, President
Volkswagen of America, Inc.
(VW, Audi, Porsche)
818 Sylvan Avenue
Englewood Cliffs, New Jersey 07632

Stig Jansson, President
Volvo Distributors, Inc.
Rockleigh, New Jersey 07647

OIL COMPANIES

Orin E. Atkins, Chairman
Ashland Oil Inc.
1401 Winchester Avenue
Ashland, Kentucky 41101

R. O. Anderson, Chairman
Atlantic Richfield Co. (Arco)
717 Fifth Avenue
New York, New York 10022

Robert Sellers, Chairman
Cities Services Co. (Citgo)
60 Wall Street
New York, New York 10005

J. G. McLean, President
Continental Oil Co. (Conoco)
30 Rockefeller Plaza
New York, New York 10020

J. P. Getty, President
Getty Oil Co.
3810 Wilshire Boulevard
Los Angeles, California 90005

B. R. Dorsey, Chief Executive Officer
Gulf Oil Corp.
Gulf Building
Pittsburgh, Pennsylvania 15219

J. C. Donnell II, President
Marathon Oil Co.
539 South Main Street
Findlay, Ohio 45840

R. Warner, Jr., Chairman
Mobil Oil Corp.
150 East 42nd Street
New York, New York 10017

W. W. Keeler, Chairman
Phillips Petroleum Co.
Bartlesville, Oklahoma 74003

D. B. Kemball-Cook, President
Shell Oil Co.
50 West 50th Street
New York, New York 10020

E. B. Miller, President
Skelly Oil Co.
1437 South Boulder Street
Tulsa, Oklahoma 74102

O. N. Miller, Chairman
Standard Oil of California (Chevron)
Standard Oil Building
San Francisco, California 94104

J. E. Swearingen, Chairman
Standard Oil of Indiana (American, Amoco)
910 South Michigan Avenue
Chicago, Illinois 60605

J. K. Jamieson, Chairman
Standard Oil Co. of New Jersey
(Humble, Esso, Enco, Exxon)
30 Rockefeller Plaza
New York, New York 10020

C. E. Spahr, Chairman
Standard Oil Co. of Ohio (Sohio)
Midland Building
Cleveland, Ohio 44115

Robert G. Dunlop, Chairman
Sun Oil Co. (Sunoco)
1608 Walnut Street
Philadelphia, Pennsylvania 19103

Maurice "Butch" Granville, Chairman
Texaco, Inc.
135 East 42nd Street
New York, New York 10017

F. C. Hartley, President
Union Oil Co. of California
461 South Boylston Street
Los Angeles, California 90017

PETROLEUM PRODUCTS

Andy Granatelli, President
S.T.P. Corp.
125 Oakton Street
Des Plaines, Illinois 60018

SPECIALTY FRANCHISERS

AAMCO Automatic Transmissions Inc.
408 East Fourth Street
Bridgeport, Pennsylvania 19405

R. C. Firestone, Chairman
Firestone Tire & Rubber Co.
1200 Firestone
Akron, Ohio 44317

T. F. O'Neil, Chairman
General Tire & Rubber Co.
One General Street
Akron, Ohio 44309

J. W. Keener, Chairman
B. F. Goodrich Co.
277 Park Avenue
New York, New York 10017

Russell De Young, Chairman
Goodyear Tire & Rubber Co.
1144 East Market Street
Akron, Ohio 44316

Midas International Corp.
(Midas Muffler)
105 West Adams Street
Chicago, Illinois 60603

MASS MERCHANDISERS

A. G. Cohen, Chairman
E. J. Korvette
c/o Arlen Realty & Developing Corp.
450 West 33rd Street
New York, New York 10001

Edward S. Donnell, Chairman
Montgomery Ward & Co., Inc.
619 West Chicago Avenue
Chicago, Illinois 60607

W. M. Batten, Chairman
J. C. Penney Co., Inc.
1301 Avenue of the Americas
New York, New York 10019

A. M. Wood, Chairman
Sears, Roebuck & Co.
925 South Homan Avenue
Chicago, Illinois 60607

ORGANIZATIONS

American Bar Association
Consumer Affairs Committee
1255 Cook Avenue
Cleveland, Ohio 44107

241

Council of Better Business Bureaus, Inc.
1150 17th Street, N.W.
Washington, D.C. 20036

Independent Garage Owners of America
624 South Michigan Avenue
Chicago, Illinois 60605

National Automobile Dealers Association
2000 K Street, N.W.
Washington, D.C. 20006

Federal Agencies

Federal Trade Commission
Bureau of Consumer Protection
Pennsylvania Avenue at 6th Street, N.W.
Washington, D.C. 20580

Federal Trade Commission regional offices:

Room 720
730 Peachtree Street, N.E.
Atlanta, Georgia 30308

Room 2200-C
John F. Kennedy Federal Building
Government Center
Boston, Massachusetts 02203

Room 221, Federal Building
111 West Huron Street
Buffalo, New York 14202

Room 206
623 East Trade Street
Charlotte, North Carolina 28202

Room 486
Everett McKinley Dirksen Building
219 South Dearborn Street
Chicago, Illinois 60604

Room 1339
Federal Office Building
1240 East 9th Street
Cleveland, Ohio 44199

Room 13-B2
1100 Commerce Street
Dallas, Texas 75202

Room 18013
Federal Office Building
1961 Stout Street
Denver, Colorado 80202

333 Mt. Elliott Avenue
Detroit, Michigan 48207

Room 508
First Federal Savings & Loan Building
843 Fort Street Mall
Honolulu, Hawaii 98613

Room 2806
Federal Office Building
911 Walnut Street
Kansas City, Missouri 64106

Room 13209
Federal Building
11000 Wilshire Boulevard
Los Angeles, California 90024

Room 931
New Federal Building
51 Southwest First Avenue
Miami, Florida 33130

22nd Floor
Federal Building 26
Federal Plaza
New York, New York 10007

231 U.S. Courthouse
Portland, Oregon 97205

San Antonio Federal Center 3
630 South Main Avenue
San Antonio, Texas 78212

Room 1132
Bank of America Building
625 Broadway
San Diego, California 92101

450 Golden Gate Avenue
Box 36005
San Francisco, California 94102

Suite 908
Republic Building
1511 Third Avenue
Seattle, Washington 98101

Room 1414
210 North 12th Street
St. Louis, Missouri 63101

6th Floor
Gellman Building
2120 L Street, N.W.
Washington, D.C. 20037

Consumer Protection Office
633 Indiana Avenue, N.W.
Washington, D.C. 20001

National Highway Traffic Safety Administration
Defects Investigation
400 7th Street, S.W.
Washington, D.C. 20591

Senator Philip Hart
Senate Subcommittee on Antitrust and Monopoly
414 Old Senate Office Building
Washington, D.C. 20510

Virginia H. Knauer, Director
White House Office of Consumer Affairs
New Executive Office Building
Washington, D.C. 20506

244

National Consumer Groups

Ralph Nader
Center for Auto Safety
800 National Press Building
Washington, D.C. 20004

Mrs. Erma Angevine, Executive Director
Consumer Federation of America
1012 14th Street, N.W.
Washington, D.C. 20005

Consumers Union of U.S., Inc.
256 Washington Street
Mount Vernon, New York 10550

State and Local Government Agencies and Local Consumer Groups Listed State by State

ALABAMA

Alabama Consumers Association
P.O. Box 1372
Birmingham, Alabama 35201

Attorney General of Alabama
State Administration Building
Montgomery, Alabama 36104

ALASKA

Alaska Consumer Council
833 13th Street West
Anchorage, Alaska 99501

Attorney General of Alaska
Pouch "K"
State Capitol
Juneau, Alaska 99801

ARIZONA

Director, Division of Consumer Fraud
Office of Attorney General
159 State Capitol Building
Phoenix, Arizona 85007

ARKANSAS

Attorney General
Consumer Protection Division
Justice Building
Little Rock, Arkansas 72201

CALIFORNIA

American Consumers Council
9720 Wilshire Boulevard
Suite 203
Beverly Hills, California 90212

Association of California Consumers
3030 Bridgeway Building
Sausalito, California 94965

Attorney General
Consumer Fraud Section
State Office Building, Room 600
Los Angeles, California 90012

Bay Area Consumer Protection Committee
c/o Department of Justice
6000 State Building
San Francisco, California 94102

The Citizen Advocate Office
Byron Bloch, Director
P.O. Box 49867
West Los Angeles, California 90049

Citizens for Consumer Action
4230 De Costa Avenue
Sacramento, California 95821

Consumer Alliance
P.O. Box 11773
Palo Alto, California 94306

Consumer Protection Committee of the City of Los Angeles
City Hall, Room 303
Los Angeles, California 90013

Bureau of Automotive Repair
Department of Consumer Affairs
1020 N Street
Sacramento, California 95814

Santa Clara County
Department of Consumer Affairs
409 Mathew Street
Santa Clara, California 95050

Division of Consumer Affairs
Ventura County
608 El Rio Drive
Oxnard, California 93030

Los Angeles Consumer Protection Committee
11000 Wilshire Boulevard
Los Angeles, California 90024

COLORADO

Attorney General
Colorado Office of Consumer Affairs
Department of Law
503 Farmers Union Building
1575 Sherman Street
Denver, Colorado 80203

Colorado Consumers Association, Inc.
P.O. Box 989
Boulder, Colorado 80302

Colorado League of Consumer Protection
8230 West 16th Place
Lakewood, Colorado 80215

CONNECTICUT

Attorney General of Connecticut
Capitol Annex
30 Trinity Place
Hartford, Connecticut 06115

Connecticut Citizen Action Group
57 Farmington Avenue
Hartford, Connecticut 06105

Connecticut Consumer Association, Inc.
One Lafayette Circle
Bridgeport, Connecticut 06603

Commissioner
Department of Consumer Protection
State Office Building
Hartford, Connecticut 06115

DELAWARE

Attorney General of Delaware
Consumer Protection Division
1206 King Street
Wilmington, Delaware 19801

Department of Consumer Affairs
Old State House
Dover, Delaware 19901

Director
Division of Consumer Affairs
704 Delaware Avenue
Wilmington, Delaware 19801

District of Columbia

City Hall Complaint Center
Office of Community Services
14th and E Streets, N.W.
Washington, D.C. 20004

Consumer Association of the District of Columbia
328 D Street, N.E.
Washington, D.C. 20002

D.C. Citywide Consumer Council
745 50th Street, N.E.
Washington, D.C. 20019

George Washington University
Consumer Protection Center
Room 3 Harlan-Brewer House
714 21st Street, N.W.
Washington, D.C. 20006

Neighborhood Consumer Information Center
Howard University
3005 Georgia Avenue
Washington, D.C. 20001

Consumer Protection Branch
United Planning Organization
1344 Maryland Avenue, N.E.
Washington, D.C. 20002

U.S. Attorney's Office
Consumer Fraud Unit
U.S. Courthouse
Constitution and John Marshall Place
Washington, D.C. 20001

Florida

American Consumer Association
P.O. Box 24141
Fort Lauderdale, Florida 33307

Attorney General of Florida
The Capitol
Tallahassee, Florida 32304

Division of Consumer Affairs
City of Jacksonville
Department of Public Safety
220 East Bay Street
Jacksonville, Florida 32202

Director of Consumer Affairs
City of St. Petersburg
264 First Avenue, N.
St. Petersburg, Florida 33701

Consumer Protection Division
Dade County
1351 Northwest 12th Street
Miami, Florida 33125

Consumers Affairs Council
208 Southeast 3rd Avenue
Fort Lauderdale, Florida 33312

Director of Consumer Services
Department of Agriculture and Consumer Services
The Capitol
Tallahassee, Florida 32304

Florida Consumers Association, Inc.
Box 3552
Tallahassee, Florida 32303

GEORGIA

Attorney General
132 State Judicial Building
Atlanta, Georgia 30334

Georgia Consumer Council
Box 311
Morris Brown College
Atlanta, Georgia 30314

Georgia Consumer Services Program
15 Peachtree Street, Room 909
Atlanta, Georgia 30303

HAWAII

Attorney General of Hawaii
Honolulu, Hawaii 96813

Director of Consumer Protection
Office of the Governor
P.O. Box 3767
Honolulu, Hawaii 96811

IDAHO

Attorney General
Consumer Protection Division
State Capitol
Boise, Idaho 83702

ILLINOIS

Attorney General of Illinois
Consumer Fraud Section
134 North LaSalle Street
Room 204
Chicago, Illinois 60602

Chicago Consumer Protection Committee
Room 486
U.S. Courthouse and Federal Building
219 South Dearborn Street
Chicago, Illinois 60604

Chicago Department of Consumer Sales
City Hall
121 North LaSalle Street
Chicago, Illinois 60602

Cook County Consumer Fraud Bureau
160 North LaSalle Street
Chicago, Illinois 60601

Illinois Citizens for Automobile Safety
5445 Hyde Park Boulevard
Chicago, Illinois 60615

Illinois Federation of Consumers
53 West Jackson Boulevard
Chicago, Illinois 60604

Students for Consumer Protection
P.O. Box 443
Rockford, Illinois 61105

INDIANA

Attorney General of Indiana
Office of Consumer Protection
219 State House
Indianapolis, Indiana 46204

Consumer Advisory Council
c/o Indiana Department of Commerce
336 State House
Indianapolis, Indiana 46204

Consumers Association of Indiana, Inc.
910 North Delaware Street
Indianapolis, Indiana 46202

IOWA

Attorney General of Iowa
Consumer Protection Division
20 East 13th Court
Des Moines, Iowa 50319

Iowa Consumers League
P.O. Box 1076
Des Moines, Iowa 50311

KANSAS

Consumer Frauds Division
Office of Attorney General
The Capitol
Topeka, Kansas 66612

Consumer Protection Division
Sedgwick County
Courthouse
Wichita, Kansas 67203

Consumer United Program
8410 West Highway 54
Wichita, Kansas 67209

Kansas City Consumer Association
7720 West 61st Street
Shawnee Mission, Kansas 66202

KENTUCKY

Attorney General of Kentucky
Consumer Protection Division
State Capitol
Frankfort, Kentucky 40601

Chairman
Citizens' Commission for Consumer Protection
State Capitol
Frankfort, Kentucky 40601

Consumer Association of Kentucky, Inc.
4515 Bishop Lane
Louisville, Kentucky 40218

Division of Consumer Affairs
City of Louisville
Metropolitan Sewer District Building
Louisville, Kentucky 40202

253

LOUISIANA

Attorney General
State Capitol
Baton Rouge, Louisiana 70804

Louisiana Consumers' League
P.O. Box 1332
Baton Rouge, Louisiana 70821

New Orleans Consumer Protection Committee
1000 Masonic Temple Building
333 St. Charles Street
New Orleans, Louisiana 70130

MAINE

Attorney General's Office
Consumer Protection Division
State House
Augusta, Maine 04330

MARYLAND

Attorney General
Consumer Protection Division
One Charles Center
Baltimore, Maryland 21201

Executive Secretary
Consumer Protection Commission
Prince Georges County
Courthouse
Upper Marlboro, Maryland 20870

Maryland Auto Safety Research Center
37 Reckford Armory
University of Maryland
College Park, Maryland 20740

Maryland Consumers Association, Inc.
P.O. Box 143
Annapolis, Maryland 21404

Montgomery County Consumer Protection Office
24 South Perry Street
Rockville, Maryland 20850

MASSACHUSETTS

Boston Consumers' Council
218 Weld Avenue
West Roxbury, Massachusetts 02119

Boston Metropolitan Consumer Protection Committee
c/o Federal Trade Commission
J. F. Kennedy Federal Building
Government Center
Boston, Massachusetts 02203

Consumer Protection Division
Department of the Attorney General
State House
Boston, Massachusetts 02133

Massachusetts Consumer Association
27 School Street
Boston, Massachusetts 02108

Massachusetts Consumers' Council
State Office Building
100 Cambridge Street
Boston, Massachusetts 02202

MICHIGAN

Attorney General
Consumer Protection Division
The Capitol
Lansing, Michigan 48903

Detroit Consumer Protection Committee
333 Mt. Elliott Avenue
Detroit, Michigan 48207

Interagency Consumer Commission
Office of the Mayor
City Hall
Detroit, Michigan 48226

Chairman
Michigan Consumer Council
525 Hollister Building
Lansing, Michigan 48933

Special Assistant to the Governor for Consumer Affairs
1033 South Washington Street
Lansing, Michigan 48910

MINNESOTA

Attorney General
Consumer Division
102 State Capitol
St. Paul, Minnesota 55101

Complaints, Inc.
Michael Kane
3343 East Calhoun
Minneapolis, Minnesota 55408

Office of Consumer Services
Department of Commerce
Room 230, State Office Building
St. Paul, Minnesota 55101

Minnesota Consumers League
P.O. Box 3063
St. Paul, Minnesota 55101

MISSISSIPPI

Attorney General
Consumer Protection Division
State Capitol
Jackson, Mississippi 39201

Consumer Protection Division
Department of Agriculture and Commerce
Jackson, Mississippi 39205

Mississippi Consumer Association
1601 Terrace Road
Cleveland, Mississippi 38732

MISSOURI

Citizens Consumer Advisory Committee
7701 Forsyth Boulevard
Clayton, Missouri 63104

Executive Director
Office of Consumer Affairs
Department of Welfare
St. Louis, Missouri 63103

Kansas City Consumer Association
940 South Woodland Drive
Kansas City, Missouri 64118

Missouri Association of Consumers
P.O. Box 514
Columbia, Missouri 65201

Consumer Protection Division
Office of the Attorney General
Supreme Court Building
Jefferson, Missouri 65101

St. Louis Consumer Federation
6321 Darlow Drive
St. Louis, Missouri 63123

MONTANA

Administrative Assistant to the Governor
The Capitol
Helena, Montana 59601

Montana Consumer Affairs Council
301 West Lawrence
Helena, Montana 59601

NEBRASKA

Attorney General
State Capitol
Lincoln, Nebraska 68509

NEVADA

Attorney General
Supreme Court Building
Carson City, Nevada 89701

NEW HAMPSHIRE

Attorney General of New Hampshire
State House Annex
Concord, New Hampshire 03301

Chairman
New Hampshire Consumer Council
8 Pepperidge Drive
Manchester, New Hampshire 03103

NEW JERSEY

Attorney General of New Jersey
State House Annex
Trenton, New Jersey 08625

Camden County Office of Consumer Affairs
Commerce Building #1 Broadway
Camden, New Jersey 08101

Consumers League of New Jersey
20 Church Street
Montclair, New Jersey 07042

Executive Director
Office of Consumer Protection
Department of Law and Public Safety
1100 Raymond Boulevard
Newark, New Jersey 07102

New Mexico

Albuquerque Consumers Association
4844 Southern Avenue, S.E.
Albuquerque, New Mexico 87108

Director
Consumer Protection Division
Attorney General's Office
Supreme Court Building, Box 2246
Santa Fe, New Mexico 87501

New York

Attorney General
The Capitol
Albany, New York 12225

Consumer Protection Board
380 Madison Avenue
New York, New York 10017

Consumer Affairs
City of Long Beach
City Hall
Long Beach, New York 11561

Metropolitan New York Consumer Council
1710 Broadway
New York, New York 10019

Commissioner
Office of Consumer Affairs
Nassau County
160 Old Country Road
Mineola, New York 11501

Bess Myerson Grant, Commissioner
City of New York Department of Consumer Affairs
80 Lafayette Street
New York, New York 10013

Consumer Frauds and Protection Bureau
Office of Attorney General
80 Centre Street
New York, New York 10013

Office of Consumer Affairs
County of Orange
Goshen, New York 10924

Consumer Assembly of Greater New York, Inc.
c/o United Housing Foundation
465 Grand Street
New York, New York 10002

Consumer Council of Monroe County
P.O. Box 3209, Federal Station
Rochester, New York 14614

NORTH CAROLINA

Attorney General
Department of Justice Building
Consumer Protection Division
P.O. Box 629
Raleigh, North Carolina 27602

North Carolina Consumers Council
108 East Jefferson Street
Monroe, North Carolina 28110

260

NORTH DAKOTA

Attorney General
Consumer Fraud Division
State Capitol
Bismarck, North Dakota 58501

OHIO

Chief
Consumer Frauds and Crimes Section
Attorney General's Office
State House Annex
Columbus, Ohio 43215

Auto Safety Research Center—Cleveland
Room 102, Case Main
10900 Euclid Avenue
Cleveland, Ohio 44106

City Sealer of Weights and Measures
City Hall
Columbus, Ohio 43215

Consumer Conference of Greater Cincinnati
318 Terrace Avenue
Cincinnati, Ohio 44114

Consumers League of Ohio
940 Engineers Building
Cleveland, Ohio 45402

Cleveland Consumer Protection Association
Mall Building, 118 St. Clair Avenue
Cleveland, Ohio 45402

Ohio Consumers Association
P.O. Box 1559
Columbus, Ohio 43216

OKLAHOMA

Attorney General
112 State Capitol
Oklahoma City, Oklahoma 73105

Consumers Council of Oklahoma
240 East Apache
Tulsa, Oklahoma 74107

Department of Consumer Affairs
Lincoln Office Plaza, Suite 74
4545 Lincoln Boulevard
Oklahoma City, Oklahoma 73105

OREGON

Assistant to the Governor for Consumer Services
State Capitol Building
Salem, Oregon 97301

Attorney General
Consumer Protection
322 State Office Building
Salem, Oregon 97310

Metropolitan Consumer Protection Agency
Multnomah County
Court House
Portland, Oregon 97204

Oregon Consumer League
919 Northwest 19th Avenue
Portland, Oregon 97232

PENNSYLVANIA

Allegheny County
Bureau of Consumer Protection
209 Jones Law Building Annex
Pittsburgh, Pennsylvania 15212

Alliance for Consumer Protection
5700 Bunkerhill Street #1002
Pittsburgh, Pennsylvania 15206

Consumers Education and Protective Association
6048 Ogontz Avenue
Philadelphia, Pennsylvania 19141

Model Cities Community
Consumer Protection Program
1521 West Girard Avenue
Philadelphia, Pennsylvania 19130

National Student Consumer Protection Council
c/o Professor A. S. Butkys
Villanova University
Villanova, Pennsylvania 19085

Director
Bureau of Consumer Protection
Pennsylvania Department of Justice
2 North Market Square
Harrisburg, Pennsylvania 17101

Pennsylvania League for Consumer Protection
P.O. Box 948
Harrisburg, Pennsylvania 17108

Consumer Services
City of Philadelphia
City Hall, Room 210
Philadelphia, Pennsylvania 19106

Philadelphia Consumer Protection Committee
53 Long Lane
Upper Darby, Pennsylvania 19082

RHODE ISLAND

Attorney General
Consumer Affairs Section
Providence County Court House
Providence, Rhode Island 02903

Executive Director
Rhode Island Consumer Council
365 Broadway
Providence, Rhode Island 02902

Rhode Island Consumers' League
131 Washington Street
Providence, Rhode Island 02903

SOUTH CAROLINA

Attorney General
Hampton Office Building
Columbia, South Carolina 29201

SOUTH DAKOTA

Attorney General
Office of Consumer Affairs
The Capitol
Pierre, South Dakota 57501

South Dakota Consumers League
Sturgis, South Dakota 50039

TENNESSEE

Executive Director
Advisory Commission on Consumer Protection
Nashville, Tennessee 37219

Attorney General
Supreme Court Building
Nashville, Tennessee 37219

Tennessee Consumer Alliance
P.O. Box 12352, Acklen Station
Nashville, Tennessee 37212

TEXAS

Attorney General
Anti-Trust & Consumer Protection Division
Supreme Court Building
Austin, Texas 78711

Commissioner of Consumer Credit
1011 San Jacinto
P.O. Box 2107
Austin, Texas 78767

Texas Consumer Association
P.O. Box 13191
Austin, Texas 78711

UTAH

Administrator of Consumer Credit
403 State Capitol
Salt Lake City, Utah 84114

Attorney General
Consumer Protection Section
236 Capitol Building
Salt Lake City, Utah 84114

League of Utah Consumers
c/o Utah Credit Union League
1706 Major Street
Salt Lake City, Utah 84115

VERMONT

Attorney General
Consumer Protection Bureau
94 Church Street
Burlington, Vermont 05401

Vermont Consumers' Association
72 Lakewood Parkway
Burlington, Vermont 05401

VIRGINIA

Arlington County Consumer
Protection Office
2049 North 15th Street
Arlington, Virginia 22201

Attorney General
Supreme Court, Library Building
Richmond, Virginia 23219

Fairfax County Consumer Protection Commission
4100 Chain Bridge Road
Fairfax, Virginia 22030

Special Assistant to the Governor for Consumer Affairs
Office of the Governor
Richmond, Virginia 23219

Virginia Beach Consumer Protection Officer
Bureau of Consumer Protection
City Hall
Virginia Beach, Virginia 23456

Virginia Citizens Consumer Council
P.O. Box 3103
Alexandria, Virginia 22303

Office of Consumer Affairs
Virginia Department of Agriculture and Commerce
8th Street Office Building
Richmond, Virginia 23219

WASHINGTON

Attorney General
Consumer Protection Division
1266 Dexter Horton Building
Seattle, Washington 98104

Washington Committee on Consumer Interests
2700 First Avenue
Seattle, Washington 98121

WEST VIRGINIA

Attorney General
State Capitol
Charleston, West Virginia 25305

Consumer Protection Division
West Virginia Department of Labor
1900 Washington Street East
Charleston, West Virginia 25305

West Virginia Consumer Association
410 12th Avenue
Huntington, West Virginia 25701

WISCONSIN

Attorney General
Office of Consumer Protection
The Capitol
Madison, Wisconsin 53702

Center for Consumer Affairs
University of Wisconsin, Milwaukee
600 West Kilbourn Avenue
Milwaukee, Wisconsin 53203

Madison Consumer League
117 West Main Street
Madison, Wisconsin 53703

Wisconsin Consumers League
P.O. Box 1531
Madison, Wisconsin 53701

WYOMING

Attorney General
120 Capitol Building
Cheyenne, Wyoming 82001

Administrator
Consumer Credit Code
State Supreme Court Building
Cheyenne, Wyoming 82001

PUERTO RICO

Attorney General
P.O. Box 192
San Juan, Puerto Rico 00902

Consumer Services Administration
P.O. Box 13934
Santurce, Puerto Rico 00908

VIRGIN ISLANDS

Public Services Commission
Charlotte Amalie
St. Thomas, Virgin Islands 00801

CANADA

L. P. Edmonston, President
Automobile Protection Association
P.O. Box 117, Station E
Montreal 151
Quebec, Canada

Consumers Association of Canada
100 Gloucester Street
Ottawa 4, Ontario
Canada

Department of Consumer and Corporate Affairs
219 Laurier Avenue West
Ottawa, Ontario KIA OC9
Canada

Appendix 4: Small Claims Courts in the U.S.

STATE	NAME OF COURT	WHERE LOCATED	MAXIMUM AMOUNT OF SUIT	ARE LAWYERS ORDINARILY ALLOWED?	IS COURT PROCEDURE INFORMAL?	WHO CAN APPEAL? PLAINTIFF	WHO CAN APPEAL? DEFENDANT	ROUGHLY WHAT DOES IT COST TO SUE?
Alabama	County Court, Court of Common Pleas, or Civil Court	County seats	$ 200 to $1500	Yes	Yes	Yes	Yes	$ 3 to $5
Alaska	District Court	Larger towns	$3000	Yes	Yes	Yes	Yes	$11 to $15
Arizona	Justice Court	County seats	$ 500	Yes	No	Yes	Yes	$ 5 to $10
Arkansas	Municipal Court	Most towns	$ 300	Yes	Yes	Yes	Yes	$15
California	Small Claims Branch of Municipal or Justice Court	Larger towns	$ 300	No	Yes	No	Yes	$ 5
Colorado	No small claims court	—	—	—	—	—	—	—
Connecticut	Small Claims Div. of Circuit Court	Many towns	$ 750	Yes	Yes	No	No	$ 3
Delaware	Justice of the Peace or Magistrate's Court	Most towns	$1500	Yes	Yes	Yes	Yes	$10
District of Columbia	Small Claims Branch of Court of General Sessions	Washington	$ 750	Yes	Yes	No	No	$ 2

State	Court	Where held	Money limit					Fee
Florida	Small Claims Court, Court of Record, or Magistrate's Court	County seats and larger towns	$250 to $1500	Yes	Yes	Yes	Yes	$3 to $10
Georgia	Small Claims Court, Justice of the Peace, or Recorder Court	County seats	$100 to $1000	Yes	Yes	Yes	Yes	$2 to $15
Hawaii	District Court	Each Island	$300	Yes	Yes	Yes	Yes	$7 to $8
Idaho	Small Claims Court or Justice Court. Magistrates Div. of District Court	Larger towns / County seats	$200	No	Yes	Yes	Yes	$5
Illinois	Circuit Court	County seats	$1000	Yes	No	Yes	Yes	$7.50
Indiana	No small claims court (see notes)	—	—	—	—	—	—	—
Iowa	Conciliation or Small Claims Court, Div. of Municipal Court (see notes)	Larger cities	$100	Yes	Yes	No	No	$3
Kansas	Magistrate Court	Larger cities	$500 to $3000	Yes	Yes	Yes	Yes	$5 to $15

NOTES: Reprinted, by permission, from *Consumer Reports* (October 1971).

Indiana. No nationwide system of small claims courts. Hancock county has an experimental county court in Greenfield authorized by state law to hear claims of $10 to $750 and to use informal procedures.

Iowa. If parties can't agree on a settlement in conciliation court, case goes to trial under strict court rules, making an attorney almost essential.

Missouri. Analysis of a few consumer complaints in Kansas City suggests consumer plaintiffs in magistrate court generally are represented by attorneys.

New York. In large cities litigants may choose arbitration instead of trial. Arbitrator's decision cannot be appealed.

Ohio. Every case goes first to conciliation court, where 80 percent are settled; others go to trial.

Pennsylvania. Arbitration is compulsory in Philadelphia; arbitrator's decision can be appealed.

Wyoming. Sometime in 1972 County Courts will replace most Justice of the Peace Courts.

Small Claims Courts in the U.S. (continued)

STATE	NAME OF COURT	WHERE LOCATED	MAXIMUM AMOUNT OF SUIT	ARE LAWYERS ORDINARILY ALLOWED?	IS COURT PROCEDURE INFORMAL?	WHO CAN APPEAL? PLAINTIFF	WHO CAN APPEAL? DEFENDANT	ROUGHLY WHAT DOES IT COST TO SUE?
Kentucky	Magistrate's Court, Justice Court, or Justice of the Peace	Most towns	$ 500	Yes	No	Yes	Yes	$ 3
Louisiana	City Court or Parish Court	Parish seat	$1000	Yes	Yes	Yes	Yes	$ 1 to $20
Maine	Small Claims Div. of District Court	County seats and larger towns	$ 200	Yes	Yes	Yes	Yes	$ 3
Maryland	District Court	County seats and larger towns	$5000	Yes	Yes	Yes	Yes	$ 4 to $13
Massachusetts	District Court	Larger towns	$ 300	Yes	Yes	Yes	Yes	$ 1.78
Michigan	Conciliation Div., Detroit Court of Common Pleas.	Detroit	$ 300	No	Yes	No	No	$ 8.50
Minnesota	District Court Conciliation Court	Larger towns County seats	$ 300 $ 300 to $550	Yes	Yes	Yes	Yes	$ 2
Mississippi	Justice of the Peace	Larger towns	$ 200	Yes	Yes	Yes	Yes	$ 6.50
Missouri	Magistrate Court (see notes)	Larger towns	$3500	Yes	Yes	Yes	Yes	$11
Montana	Justice Court	Most towns	$ 300	Yes	No	Yes	Yes	$ 7
Nebraska	No small claims court	—	—	—	—	—	—	—

272

State	Court	Location	Amount					Fee
Nevada	Small Claims Div. of Justice Court	County seat and larger towns	$ 300	No	Yes	Yes	Yes	$ 7
New Hampshire	District Court or Municipal Court	Most towns	$ 200	Yes	Yes	Yes	Yes	$ 2.68
New Jersey	Small Claims Div. of District Court	County seats	$ 200 $ 500 for rent security cases	Yes	Yes	Yes	Yes	$ 4
New Mexico	Small Claims or Magistrate's Court	Albuquerque	$2000	Yes	Yes	Yes	Yes	$14
New York	Magistrate's Court	Larger towns	$ 500	Yes	Yes	Yes	Yes	$ 3
	Small Claims Branch of Civil or City Court (see notes)	Larger cities	$ 500					
		Smaller cities	$ 500					
North Carolina	Small Claims Div. of District Court	County seats	$300	Yes	Yes	Yes	Yes	$ 3 to $6
North Dakota	Small Claims Court	County seats	$ 200	Yes	Yes	Yes	Yes	$ 3
Ohio	Small Claims Court (see notes)	County seats	$ 150	Yes	Yes	Yes	Yes	$ 2.75
Oklahoma	Small Claims Div. of County Court	County seats	$ 400	Yes	Yes	Yes	Yes	$ 8 to $10
Oregon	Small Claims Court	County seats	$ 200	No	Yes	No	No	$ 2 to $5
Pennsylvania	District Justice Court	Most towns	$ 500	Yes	Yes	Yes	Yes	$ 7.50 to $15
	Municipal Court	Philadelphia	$ 500					
	County Court (see notes)	Pittsburgh	$ 500					

Small Claims Courts in the U.S. (continued)

STATE	NAME OF COURT	WHERE LOCATED	MAXIMUM AMOUNT OF SUIT	ARE LAWYERS ORDINARILY ALLOWED?	IS COURT PROCEDURE INFORMAL?	WHO CAN APPEAL? PLAINTIFF	DEFENDANT	ROUGHLY WHAT DOES IT COST TO SUE?
Rhode Island	Small Claims Div. of District Court	Larger towns	$ 300	Yes	Yes	No	Yes	$ 1.57
South Carolina	Court of Magistrate	Most towns	$ 100	Yes	Yes	Yes	Yes	no fee
South Dakota	Municipal Court or Justice of the Peace.	Most towns	$ 500	Yes	Yes	Yes	Yes	$ 2
Tennessee	District Court / Civil Div., Court of General Sessions	County seats / County seats	$ 500 / $3000	Yes	Yes	Yes	Yes	$8.75
Texas	Justice of the Peace	Most towns	$ 200	Yes	Yes	No	Yes	$ 5 to $7.50
Utah	City Court or Justice of the Peace	Larger towns	$ 200	Yes	Yes	Yes	Yes	$ 6
Vermont	Small Claims Div. of District Court	Most towns	$ 250	Yes	Yes	No	No	under $5
Virginia	Civil Court or County Court	Most towns	$ 300 to $3000	Yes	Yes	Yes	Yes	$ 5
Washington	Small Claims Div. of Justice Court	County seats	$ 200	No	Yes	No	Yes	$ 2 to $5
West Virginia	Justice of the Peace	Most towns	$ 300	Yes	Yes	Yes	Yes	$ 5
Wisconsin	Small Claims Branch of County Court	County seats	$ 500	Yes	Yes	Yes	Yes	$ 4.50
Wyoming	Justice of the Peace (see notes)	Most towns	$ 200	Yes	Yes	Yes	Yes	$ 6

Glossary

accelerator linkage adjustment—an adjustment of the levers that connect the gas pedal to the carburetor. A careful adjustment of this is very important to make sure the gas pedal doesn't stick open.

alternator—a modern type of generator. *See* generator.

axles—the solid rods on which the wheels spin.

ball joints—the joints on which the front wheels swivel for steering; made of a ball in a socket.

bands—metal belts in the transmission which tighten to transmit power.

battery—a device that stores electrical energy for starting the engine.

brake drums—the hollow part of the car wheels on which the brake shoes rub.

brake fluid—a liquid that transmits the force from the brake pedal to the brake shoes by pressure.

brake shoes—the brake parts which rub or drag to stop the car.

carburetor—the part on top of the engine which mixes gas and air.

coil—an electrical part which generates the very high voltages needed for the spark plugs.

condenser—an electrical part necessary for spark production.

crankcase—the metal pan that covers the bottom of the engine.

crankshaft—the cranklike part which converts the up-down motion of the pistons into a spinning motion.

cylinders—the hollow chambers in the engine where the explosions take place.

differential—the gears that transmit the longitudinal spinning of the drive shaft to the sideward spinning of the rear axle. Known also as the Hotchkiss Drive.

distributor—a rotating switch above the points which connects the spark voltage to the proper spark plug in sequence.

distributor cap—the plastic cover on the distributor.

drive shaft—the long spinning shaft which connects the transmission with the rear axle.

ethylene glycol—a chemical (antifreeze) that is added to the radiator water to prevent its freezing.

exhaust manifold—the pipes that carry the exhaust gases from the cylinder to the exhaust pipe.

generator—the device that generates electricity to charge the battery.

hydrometer—an instrument that measures the concentration of antifreeze or battery fluid.

intake manifold—the passageway through which the atomized gas travels when going from the carburetor to the cylinders.

muffler—the exhaust system chamber which deadens the sound of the engine.

PCV valve—a valve that regulates the flow of polluted air from the crankcase to the intake manifold.

pistons—the plungerlike parts which are pushed up and down in the cylinders by the explosions.

piston rods—the rods that connect the pistons to the crankshaft.

points—a switch that is opened and closed as the engine turns and which controls spark production.

seals—the softer materials which are used between metal parts to prevent leaks.

solenoid—the electrically operated switch which turns on the heavy rush of current needed by the starter motor.

spark plugs—the parts that produce sparks in the cylinders.

starter motor—an electric motor that spins the engine to start it.

tie rods—the rods that connect the front wheels with the steering column mechanism and transmit the turning forces.

transmission—the box of gears behind the engine which allows the engine to run at somewhat the same speed whether the car is going fast or very slow.

U-joints or universal joints—the joints that allow flexing in the drive shaft.

vacuum modulator—a unit that adjusts the time of the sparks depending on the operating mode of the engine (decelerating, accelerating, etc.).

valves—the holes in the top of each cylinder which open to let the gas-air mixture in and the exhaust out.

water pump—the pump that circulates the cooling water.

Whatever Happened to the Backyard Fence?

As a means of passing valuable information between neighbors, including gossip on such breakthroughs as the Model-T and the inflatable tire, the backyard fence was unsurpassed.

Americans still enjoy sharing secrets and consumer finds. It's just that spreading this knowledge person to person isn't very efficient.

Good information is especially hard to find in the field of auto repair. Everyone has at one time asked a friend, "Do you know a good, honest mechanic?"

In partnership with Consumers Union (publisher of the respected *Consumer Reports*) and Ralph Nader's Center for Auto Safety, the author plans to help fill this information gap.

We are establishing the Auto Repair Institute which will catalog and rate car repair facilities in much the same manner that Michelin rates restaurants. Instead of stars, we'll use wrenches. Four wrenches means a first-rate garage. Three and two wrenches indicate a lesser degree of competence. A one-wrench garage means "Use only in emergency and watch like a hawk." The British already have a garage rating system of this kind.

How will we collect the information? First, the Center for Auto Safety has received more than 20,000 letters from car owners around the country. Many contain complaints or compliments about local car repair facilities. This information is being cataloged for our use.

Second, we will tap the consumer agencies in such big cities as New York, Chicago, and Los Angeles which have accumulated extensive files on local gyp artists as well as the mechanics who do a good job.

Finally, we are asking the help of our readers. Fill out the form on the other side of this page, tear it out, and mail to:
Auto Repair Institute
923 15th Street, N.W.
Washington, D.C. 20005
Make this form your backyard fence.

277

YOUR
  NAME _____

ADDRESS _____

NAME OF
  GARAGE _____

ADDRESS _____

MAKE, MODEL, AND
  YEAR OF CAR _____
REPAIRS
  REQUESTED _____ ESTIMATE _____
REPAIRS
  PERFORMED _____ FINAL BILL _____
OVERALL
  RATING (Check one): __ Good __ Fair __ Poor
REASON FOR
  YOUR RATING: _____
CAN YOU DOCUMENT YOUR COMPLAINT (OLD
  PARTS, REPAIR ORDER, ETC.)?